Sex Up Your Life

*20+ Key Secrets to Unleashing Her
Inner Slut*

Richard Master

Editing by Carrie Cassidy

ISBN: 193863408X
ISBN-13: 978-1-938634-08-6

SEX UP YOUR LIFE
By Richard Master

For more books like this one, visit Richard
Master's website at:
http://richardmaster.com/

2013 copyright by Freedom of Speech Publishing,
Inc.

Printed in the United States of America
The publisher offers discounts on this book when
ordered in bulk quantities. For more information,
contact Sales Department, Phone 815-290-9605,
Email:
sales@FreedomOfSpeechPublishing.com

Freedom of Speech Publishing, Leawood KS,
66224
www.FreedomOfSpeechPublishing.com
ISBN: 193863408X
ISBN-13: 978-1-938634-08-6

A SPECIAL THANK YOU TO YOU!

On behalf of everyone at Freedom Of Speech Publishing, thank you for choosing Sex Up Your Life for your reading enjoyment.

As an added bonus and special thank you, for purchasing Sex Up Your Life, you can enjoy discounts and special promotions on other Freedom of Speech Publishing products. Visit www.freedomeofspeech.com/vip to learn more.

We are committed to providing you with the highest level of customer satisfaction possible. If for any reason you have questions or comments, we are delighted to hear from you. Email us at cs@freedomofspeechpublishing.com or visit our website at: http://freedomofspeechpublishing.com/contact-us-2/.

If you enjoyed Sex Up Your Life, visit www.freedomofspeechpublishing.com for a list of similar books or upcoming books.

Again, thank you for your patronage. We look forward to providing you more entertainment in the future.

Acknowledgements

First, I'd like to thank my friends John, Chuck, and Joe for contributing your successes and failures while trying to get laid. Hell, some of the contributions were about what to do and what not to do WHILE getting laid. So, thank you for the valuable information.

Next, I'd like to thank my editor Carrie Cassidy who added her valuable editing experience to this book. We had several conversations while she was editing this book that involved me asking her, what did you think about when you read that chapter. I love criticism and she helped me a ton.

Thank you to Alexis Star who helped by writing the Foreword for this book. I really appreciate your efforts.

Dedication

I would like to dedicate this book first to the men that will learn and benefit from the experiences shown in the book. I would also like to dedicate the book to the beautiful women that will also benefit from the great sex they are about to get!

Contents

Foreword

Only someone with Richard Master's experience could write about sexual pursuit and strategies for seducing women with this much expertise. The decades he has spent practicing the art of seduction are evident not just in the first hand stories he shares throughout the book, but also in the wisdom he shares on every page. You can tell from the very first page by his no-nonsense approach, Richard knows what he's talking about when it comes to attracting and impressing women in any situation.

What's most impressive about this book is his courage to tell it like it is. Richard doesn't mince words. Early in the book he tells us, "The information you're about to read, will spell it all out," and he proceeds to do exactly that. He takes no prisoners, confronting men and women alike on their flawed thinking. He explains in detail why your current strategy isn't getting you where you want to be. As a single woman and someone who loves to meet good-looking men, I consider myself a bit of an expert in this area. I was surprised when I was noticeably affected as I read and discovered many tips I could apply to my own life. I have used just about every coy technique Richard exposes in an attempt to keep men from seeing right to the core of my inner struggle between good girl and slut. Page by page I was forced to face the reality, that once this book hits the market, I'm no longer going to be able to count on my time-tested techniques that have kept the men in my life wrapped around my little finger. I even found myself saying aloud, "Hey Richard, you're really pissing me off here!" I mean who does this guy think he is publishing a book that will make it harder for women everywhere to conceal our sexual desires? He's got his facts straight, his knowledge is extensive, and I suspect this book will change the dating game forever.

There are countless parts of this book that stand out, but I'll just whet your appetite with a couple of my favorites. Richard has the courage to tell any guy straight-up, that if you're not getting laid, it's your own damn fault. No candy coating for your male ego, or allowing for excuses in order to soften his message. He's got the facts straight about what it takes to succeed with women. If you're looking for a kind and gentle nudge in the right direction, this may not be the book for you. If you want hard hitting, guaranteed methods to improve your prowess with the ladies, you really can't afford not to read this book.

Richard pulls no punches as he explains why simply wanting to have sex with a woman is not enough. You've got to work at evaluating yourself, and correcting your weaknesses. His advice is right on with tips about hygiene, clothes, conversation and even how to correctly touch a woman when it's time to turn up the heat. I must admit I could feel myself squirming a bit as he described his techniques for kissing and caressing a woman's body. Trust me, based on the tingles I was feeling reading this part of the book, the author knows exactly what buttons to push to make a woman want him. If you've always wondered what makes women like me go from, "absolutely not" to "oh my god", you'll want to be sure to pay close attention.

I've read quite a few books and articles covering the exact topics that Richard tackles here in his book. I'm always curious to find out if the unspoken rules of seduction have actually been publically revealed. After every book and article I've read, I've been relieved to find out that yet another man doesn't know what the hell he's talking about. Frankly, I don't know where some of these author's even come up with a lot of the nonsense they spew. Strange pick-up lines and awkward small talk certainly don't get my mood headed in a sexy direction.

Well, by the time I reached the end of Richard's book, I knew it was going to be game over for thousands of women across America and around the world. This guy has broken the code and exposed the secrets that women don't want men to know. Now every trick and technique I count on to keep men guessing and making fools of themselves is being shared with the world. So guys, fasten your seatbelts and enjoy the ride. This book is your ticket out of a sex-starved way of life. Read the pages that follow, and your seduction skills will go from so-so to stellar.

~ Alexis Starr

Chapter 1 – How to use this Book

When's the last time you got laid? If you've got to stop and look at a damn calendar, it's been far too long my friend. Are you frustrated? Are you pissed off? Are you tired of spending all your hard earned money on strippers and hookers? Do you really enjoy buying expensive drinks for bitches that don't give you the time of day? It's time to stop whining about it. Stop feeling sorry for yourself and start getting laid. Everything you need to trade your hand for a red-hot honey is right here for the taking.

You may be wondering just who exactly this book is written for. The truth is this book is written for everyone. There is an enormous variety of people from all walks of life who are reading this just like you are. There's not one specific type of person who seeks out my advice.

There are both men that are successful with women, and those that are painfully hopeless when it comes to getting a woman naked and into bed. Both guys buy my book for different

5

reasons. There is however, one thing both groups have in common. They are looking to step up their game and get laid. Now let's take a look at each group.

Odds are if you are a man that is already successful with women, you are turning these pages searching for those hard to obtain, secret lady-attracting tricks you know are out there. You're always on the lookout for ammunition you can add to your getting laid arsenal. Men are greedy. It's in our genetics. Even if you're getting laid every night, you're always on the hunt for more ways to guarantee you get a piece of ass when you need it. You want to know how to seduce even the hottest woman in the room. The only thing better than getting it on with a smoking-hot woman, is getting your dick wet with an even hotter woman the next night.

If you are a man that isn't successful with the ladies, you are reading this book to figure out what the hell you have been doing wrong. I can confidently tell you that your approach is all wrong. If it wasn't you'd know it, because you'd be getting some pussy. Your skills when it comes to picking up women are crap. That's why you're sitting there all by yourself night after night. You can change that starting today.

Get ready, because if you do what I tell you to do, your lonely nights are about to become a distant memory. Your life is going to change forever. Women you want to have sex with will give it up with ease. Are you ready to start getting laid without her demanding to be paid?

The information you're about to read, will spell it all out. How to finally stop being a horny bastard, and start being a ladies' man. Your whole approach is going to get flipped on its head. The results will be nothing short of amazing. When it's closing time at the bar, you will be the guy leaving with a horny woman on your arm. Forget about feeling jealous and like a failure as yet again, some other dude takes her back to his bed for some late-night fun between the sheets.

You really can make this happen. First of all though, you need to understand that it takes much more than a quick skim through a book to master the art of seduction. Be prepared to spend many nights practicing and getting comfortable with the techniques I'm about to teach you. In each chapter I'll start off by sharing specific examples that will clearly show you where you're screwing up, and why you're failing to close the deal.

Next, I'll lay out a step by step plan of action. You'll know exactly what you must do to stop getting slapped, and start spreading her legs like a champ. Expect and even be willing to embrace occasional rejection as you put each lesson into practice. I've got the answers, but you're going to have to do the work it takes to become a true pro.

Guys it may shock you, but there are women reading this book as well. More of them than you might think. Women that pick up a copy of my book do so mainly out of curiosity. That curiosity along with her bitchy self-righteous attitude draws her in like a bear to a tree full of honey. If you are a woman, you are probably rolling your eyes and smugly asking yourself right now, "What stupid shit is this guy going to say that will supposedly lure me in and let men get into my pants."

Well honey, quite frankly, if you're asking that question, you already know I'm onto your game. You're worried I may have just figured out the key to getting your panties off. Guess what? I have figured it out, and you're just going to have to deal with that. Odds are high that I'll be in your bed making you scream for more if that's what I decide is going to happen. I'm about to let thousands of men in on all of those little secrets women like you have kept under wraps for decades.

Or, because you think you're so damn smart and coy, maybe you'll do what other women before you have done, and go out and fuck the hell out of some idiot just to prove me wrong. Just to prove you're the predator and not the prey. Guess what girl? I don't care. I've already played and won all of your little games. I do hope you're cute though. That way, at least the guy you're about to bang will get to enjoy looking at your pretty face while he fucks you.

Anyways guys, as you hopefully understand by now, readers of this book come in countless shapes, and forms and flavors. That's the point I want you to get. We all need a little inspiration, a little tune up to our game from time to time. Never forget, that if you allow yourself to get too cocky, you'll be spending most of your nights alone. I don't know about you, but that's a risk I'm not willing to take. Work hard, and I guarantee you'll be the guy playing the field, and not the one sitting on the bench.

You know those super studs that are practically geniuses when it comes to women?

Sometimes they strike out. Hell, even those super-hot and sexy supermodel types we all want to bang get blown off. It's a fact. Not one single person bags their first choice every time. You're not going to be the sole exception.

However, I promise you this. You will greatly increase the amount of pussy you get if you listen to my advice, and then get out there and practice. You've got to be persistent. If a woman blows you off or attempts to make you her fool, pack it up and move on to the next one. Get up, dust yourself off, and go out there and try again. Your efforts will pay off, and your dick will thank you. Trust me.

Keep in mind that on occasion you'll run into an odd chic who doesn't want to play by the rules. Sometimes you will get rejected unexpectedly after you say something perfectly normal, or make your big move on a woman. Then next week with another woman you might say the exact same thing and get lucky. It's even happened to me.

Let's take a look at the following example. I went on a date with a cute nurse and gave her a small kiss good night. It was very harmless. She called me up later and told me I shouldn't have done that. She said I should've asked her first. There was no second date. I took a different woman out the next weekend. At the end of our date, I asked her if I could give her a kiss. She literally told me, "Dude, why are you asking me? If you want to kiss me, just do it!"

So what gives? Although the basic techniques will always remain the same, every woman is a little bit different. Each approaches sex and men in their own unique way. It takes practice to understand this. You're not going to talk to two or three women and suddenly be getting your dick wet every night. Read the book and really pay attention to everything I'm about to tell you. Then, get off the couch, put away the video games, and get your ass out there and get laid.

Chapter 2 – Women are like Geese

Have you ever noticed that women tend to congregate in groups? If you look closely, there's always one woman who is more alert than all of the others? There's a reason behind this phenomenon. Women are like geese. If you watch a group of geese in the wild, one goose always has its head up. It's tuned in and alert. That goose is constantly looking around trying to spot any potential predators. She keeps a sharp eye out for trouble so the other geese can eat in peace.

Right now you are probably saying to yourself, "What the hell does this have to do with getting laid?" Hang in here with me guys. This really is crucial information you must know to be successful at picking up women.

To women, men are the predators. In their minds they are the geese, and we men are the wolves. Just like a gathering of geese is always on the lookout for predators, groups of women are constantly scanning the room looking out for men that might be trying to intrude into their space. Women are not men, and they approach social situations in an entirely different way than we do. If you don't know how they think, you're chance of getting laid is next to nothing.

If you make your assumptions about women based on your experience reading Penthouse letters and watching porn, you are not going to get any pussy. What do I mean by this? For example let's take a look at a friend I had who believed all women just want to get drunk and whip their tops off. In his dim-witted fantasy of a world, all women happily run around flashing their tits like one of those damn Girls Gone Wild videos you see on late-night TV.

He explained to me that women just want to let it all hang out for the pleasure of us men. He also felt a girl always has a friend around just to keep her sober and stop her from indulging her natural free-spirited, tit-flashing desires. Predictably, the end result was he did terrible with women, and they avoided him like the fucking plague. They did whatever it took to stay the hell away from him, because they saw him as a dangerous predator to be avoided at all costs. By the way, as you might guess, that guy is a complete dumbass, and he is no longer my friend. The point I want you to take away is women know men want to have sex with them.

Don't think for a moment they don't know exactly what your motives are. Now this does not mean women aren't horny. They are, you just have to know how to get through the invisible wall they put up to keep you away.

So, what is that flock of women over there looking for in a man anyways? I won't lie to you, it can be hard to say, and women are damned difficult to please. At times, it can even be nearly impossible to figure out what exactly they want from a guy in order for him to get a little action. In fact, I'm convinced that sometimes a woman's behavior is impossible on purpose, just to test a man's will and find out how into them we really are!

I don't know about you, but I am not a fucking psychic or magic mind reader, no matter how much that flock of women may expect us to be. I've got some quick tips that I use that can help you out too. A few clues for the clueless among us. These are guaranteed to keep your game sharp, and to get even the most poorly behaved woman eating up your game like bird seed straight from your hand.

Women need to feel like they have permission to bring their wild side out of hiding. They are told from the time they are very young girls, it's not proper and lady like to get wild and crazy. So she believes it's not okay to get sexy. Until of course, you come along and become her excuse. All women have a wild side. Trust me! They all want an excuse to let their sexy hair down and let their inner sex kitten out of its cage. Give them that excuse by taking the lead.

No matter how much a women insists she is proper and civilized, once you show her that you think she's smoking hot when she's wild, she'll throw all that coyness out the window. She will release her wild side with a passion that will get your adrenaline pumping in your pants!

How to do it? It's simple, a woman wants a man who she feels completely at ease with. Make her feel fantastic about her mind, body and the connection you feel with her, and suddenly she'll develop an urge to nurture those thoughts and feelings In short, for you this means sexual fun and experimentation in the bedroom! Women are often far more kinky than you think, especially when they can free their minds. Take her hand and lead her over to the wild side.

Let her know that she can trust you. I'm assuming you want a happy, independent and secure woman who isn't going to smother you by being needy, am I right? Of course I am. Be upfront with her then! Never underestimate a woman, they are sensitive and highly intuitive, beautiful creatures. They know when something isn't quite right. If you want them to feel happy and relaxed and be themselves, show them they can trust you by sharing your fears and concerns. You might not think it's manly to talk about your feelings, but women don't think like that. A woman will be impressed with you if you know how to talk to her. She will also always appreciate knowing exactly where she stands. Tell her how you feel and what you think, then you can get on with enjoying each other, rather than trying to figure each other out and waste time playing mind games.

Be exciting for her to be around. Life can be boring. Why not be exciting? Teach her something new. Educating a woman is fun and sexy. Listen carefully: women are more intelligent than you. Don't get all defensive here dude. What I mean is that they are challenging, in a good way, and we love a challenge, right?

A man who can stimulate his woman's mind by showing her a different perspective to life, and challenge her thoughts and views, is a man who will keep her interested and on her toes. Share your skills, knowledge and opinions. A little arrogance (not too much) can create a sexy tension between you that she will want to play with. Most importantly, surprise her in the bedroom. Keep it fresh and alive by bringing something new to her attention. When you make an effort to keep it fresh, so will she.

Let her see how hot for her you are. She is a gift, she is gorgeous, and she deserves your full attention. No woman wants to feel taken for granted. Make her feel sexy and unique, and she will feel respected. The reward for your efforts is a happy, horny and sexy woman. Express your desire for her like you would express your hunger for food. She wants to be devoured.

Get creative too. More often than not, all a woman wants is to feel a physical and mental connection with you. So kiss her like you mean it, and not just like you want to get laid! Use your entire body, and ravish her. Look deep into her eyes. Leave her feeling breathless and wanting more. I'll be the first to admit this all sounds a little cliché, but the reason you've heard this advice everywhere is because it works.

Use the element of surprise, and surprise her whenever you get a chance. Be spontaneous and be romantic! Do not think romance is about little cupids and flowers and shit like that. Real men know that genuine romance is about paying attention to every detail. You have to show her you know exactly what she needs on an emotional level in order to feel sexy. A little effort in the romance department can make a massive difference to the excitement in your relationship and turn up the heat in your sex life. She'll be secretly super happy when you pay attention to the details, and when you tune in to who she is as a person. Listen to her, pay attention, and use those details to step up your seduction and get laid more often.

How's that for a head start? Oh sorry, did you want more detail? More specifics? More step-by-step instructions? Impossible. Women are not all the same. Make the effort to get to know what turns your chosen lady on, and what makes her feel totally connected to you. If you want to get the best sex possible from her and maximize your chance to get laid every night, this is the way to make it happen. Let's face it, bottom line, as men we want to have sex with women.

Hell, women want to have sex with men. However, if you are viewed as a potential threat to their safety because you make assumptions or crude sexual insinuations, they'll blow you off instantly. I have another example. I started a conversation with a beautiful woman that led into a brief but very good conversation. It ended because she told me she was happily married and I responded, "I don't care. I'm alright with it if you are." She gave me a really shitty look and walked away quickly.

You see, she knew I was hitting on her and wanted to have sex with her. I became a threat when I made it abundantly clear I was only interested in getting her in bed. If I really cared about getting to know this woman long term, I should've answered, "I understand, but I like talking with you." But, I didn't care and was only trying to get in her pants. It is alright to be confident, but don't be too aggressive or she'll run. Remember, women are like geese. Sometimes a goose will let you feed it, but if you try to pet it too quickly, it'll fly away.

Sometimes, you'll run into situations where you're talking to two or more women at the same time and you have an interest in only one of them. You want to make sure to include all the women in the conversation. Try to include the woman you're hot for in the conversation more than the other girls. It can be hard to manage this and will take some real effort on your part.

However, if a woman starts talking to you more than any of the others, then maybe you should focus on her. She's interested in you. She is likely to be an easy score. If you aren't interested in her, you have to get the woman you are interested in back into the conversation. Do this carefully, because if you noticed the friend is into you, how much do you want to bet her friend also picked up on it? Always find out who the lead goose is in the group. If it is the friend you're not interested in, and you are rude to her, the others will run.

It's also critical to start your hunt in the right part of the room. If you were a fox looking to catch a goose for dinner, would you start in the middle of the group or at the back of the group? If you go hunting and kill the goose farthest out away from the lead goose, the others don't get frightened and fly away. Think of women the same way. If you hit on a woman in the back of the room and she shoots you down, the only women that see it are those near her. Even though your ass just got rejected, you've still got prospects to chase. Don't feel bad or let your confidence be shaken because you've been denied. It happens. Keep moving.

Turn that rejection into excitement, and use that momentum as you move on to the next woman. Walk to the other side of the room and find another woman you're interested in. Very likely, this woman did not see you get shot down and will be forced to make her own opinion of you. This is exactly what you want. Gradually work your way in towards the middle of the room. If the woman in the middle shoots you down, you're done for the night. Everyone will see it and know you got rejected. Go home and cry a little. You've just blown it.

When you are shot down and other women see it, they inherently think the woman that shot you down knows something about you that's not good. You are a potential predator to the geese. You want to avoid this type of pre-judgment. It will make it super hard for you to get laid.

There is one exception to starting in the back of the room. If the back of the room is the women's bathroom, don't stand there. It's creepy. And, do you really want to be compared to a shit house? Women will subconsciously associate you with the bathroom, and that is not a good thing.

You don't want to stand in the same spot all night either. If you want to sit back and watch women, go to a strip club and sit in the back of the room. Just be prepared for strippers to walk up to you to ask if you're interested in buying an expensive lap dance. While we're on the topic, here's a little advice about strippers for you. When they get all in your face and pushy trying get your hard-earned cash, just tell them you're gay. They'll usually leave you the hell alone.

In the next chapter you're going to learn all about the special lady I like to call the lead goose. Let me clue you in right now, starting with the lead goose will lead to a night of rejections. Many men start with the hottest women in the room and get rejected right away. This causes the other geese to think something is wrong with you even though they haven't taken the time to talk to you. Their lead goose has already decided you are a loser. Now you may not actually be a loser, but as far as the women are concerned you are. Case closed.

If you start by talking to other women and the lead goose is remotely interested in you, she'll make an effort to let you know. Then and only then, you can talk to her. I have a friend that is extremely attractive and a picture-perfect example of the stereotypical "bad boy". He typically only starts one conversation with a woman per night with the intention of having sex with that woman later that same night. He always selects the best looking woman in the room. If she isn't interested, he gets shot down and goes home by himself. Guess what? He almost always goes home by himself. He'd be much better off if he tried instead to get laid by the women who are not in role of lead goose.

Chapter 3 – Women are VERY Competitive

Have you always assumed the male gender is the only one that thrives on competition? After all, it does make a lot of sense. Dudes play football, and girls wear short skirts, shake their pom-poms and get us off in the backseat of our dad's car right? Not so fast fellas.

There is a long and established pattern of behavior that proves women are just as competitive as men. The reason you may not have figured this out, is because the way they compare themselves is a hell of a lot different than the way us guys go about it.

Let me show you what this looks like in practice. I bet you'll be smacking yourself for not catching on sooner. The sizing up that goes on between two women happens as soon as they spot one another. Now if you don't know what I do, you won't even notice. Here's how it works.

Whenever two or more women are standing next to one another, they each immediately begin making internal comparisons. Girls start doing this way back in middle school, and it remains part of the female social norm throughout high school and all the way on into adulthood. Hot babe or homely plain Jane, they all do it all of the time.

This typically internal dialogue follows a pretty predictable course. For example, the first woman may have bigger tits and a bigger ass than the other. The woman with the big tits is thinking, "My boobs are bigger then hers, but her butt looks better than mine in that mini skirt." The woman with the smaller tits may be thinking, "My ass is so much sexier then hers. She has a fat ass. But damn it, her boobs are bigger than mine." They could be best friends and yet they will still have that constant internal mental competition going back and forth between them.

It's not even always silent. It's pretty funny, but unbelievably I've been around many times where I've actually heard women talk to each other about this shit. I've watched them going back and forth sizing up their tits and asses with each other. Sometimes an entire group of girls will be doing this. It's crazy man!

Can you imagine if guys talked like that? "Dude, your ass looks sexy in those jeans. I have a bigger dick then you do though." Weird doesn't even begin to describe what that exchange of conversation would look like. Hell, even in a room full of naked dudes, standing around comparing dicks just isn't going to happen. It's not how we as men roll. It is however, how females establish the highest-ranking girl within any group of women. It sounds ridiculous, and it is. It doesn't matter. If you want pussy, you must understand how this works. You may be laughing now, but trust me here. Let me tell you why it's no joke.

When women go out in groups, the competition is fierce. They've all got their slutty short skirts on. They've got their makeup just right, nails painted, all of that bullshit. It doesn't matter though. There is always that one woman in the group who is the hottest. It's not like the women all sit around, talk to each other and sort this out over a fucking cup of tea or something. Like I've already told you, it is most often done quickly and without a word.

Every woman knows who the hottest woman amongst them is. That woman also knows she's the hottest bitch in the joint She is aware beyond a doubt that she will be the most desired piece of ass in the room. Every man in her presence will want to take her home, pull up her skirt and bang her.

As such, this hot babe who is causing all of us guys to walk around with half a hard on is carefully looked up and down by the other women. They all know she is going to get hit on all night long, and they want a piece of that male attention pie too. Who the hell wants to be a wall flower while some other bitch gets all of the action? Not to mention all of the free drinks. So the other women will start trying to figure out how get the edge on her in some small way.

Even though they already know this other girl has outdone them, they will still try to catch your eye. You can get far more attention from them tonight than if they were the hottest girl. This only applies if you play your cards right. Don't get me wrong, none of this means there is always a single hottie, and the rest of them are dogs.

Often, hot women also have hot friends. Hot friends equal a great opportunity for you to get laid by a good looking piece of ass. Now you're probably saying, "That's great man, but are you going to tell me how to play my cards to make this happen?" Of course I am. Here's the deal.

The hottest woman in the group is always the lead goose. She has the power to give you a very good evening and a lot of success meeting other women. She also has the power to make your night very miserable and unproductive. The lead goose tends to be a bit of a ruthless bitch. It doesn't matter. You are trying to get laid not make a new best friend here. If you are ballsy enough to approach her, she may seem impressed with you. She may even seem to like you. Don't be a dumbass. If you are anyone other than Brad Pitt or his long lost brother, you should be wondering why the hell she seems to be coming onto you. The answer is, she's using you for entertainment. As soon as a better looking guy comes around, you'll be ditched.

A few years back before I knew better, I met this gorgeous blonde with long tan legs and a heart-shaped ass you would not believe. For obvious reasons, she was the lead goose in her group. We talked for several minutes, and then I asked what bar she was headed to next. She told me she was going to the local dance bar, and asked if I'd go there and dance with her. I agreed.

She left and pretty quickly after that my friend and I finished our beers and went to the dance bar to hook up with her and her friends.

When I got there, I spotted her, made my way across the room, and danced with her for one song. She happily let me grab her ass and rub my dick up against her on the dance floor. Things are looking great right? What happened next will probably blow your mind.

I didn't know it, but she had already picked out my replacement. She blew me off within minutes and began rubbing herself all over a different guy. His hands were now firmly planted on that same sweet ass mine had been just two songs before. Shit! That really sucked. What made it even worse is all the other women saw it happen. I couldn't get a conversation started with a different woman the entire rest of the night.

Once the lead goose has played with you and then rejected you, you're screwed. You're not getting laid by even the ugly bitch over in the corner you'd have to bend over to enjoy. If it's not closing time yet, your best bet is to head to a different bar and start over with a different girl before you've totally sealed your fate. Otherwise you're going to end up in the company of a box of tissues and that lame '70s porno you've watched more times than you like to admit.

When time is running out, you've got to go for the sure thing. One of my favorite ways to meet a lot of women quickly is to look for bachelorette parties. I'll go up to the bride-to-be and talk with her for a few minutes. I typically tell her I am happy for her and ask her about her upcoming wedding. After she starts to feel more comfortable with me, I ask to be introduced to her friends.

Usually, several of them are single, and at least one is a little interested in me. Most guys get intimidated and won't talk to a group of women. As I said before, there is always a hot woman in the group. You have a fighting chance with anyone but her. With bachelorette parties, whether or not the bride-to-be is hotter than the others or not, she holds that title for tonight. She is the lead goose for her group of women.

If she likes you, you have an in. You are definitely in the running to get a piece of ass from one of her bridesmaids. If she doesn't like you, nobody in the group will like you either. Just like in the earlier example, getting the brush off from the lead goose is a guarantee you're not getting action from any of the women in her gaggle.

Chapter 4 – Look the Part You WANT to Play

People tend to take their personal appearance for granted. I know I used to. After a few incidents with the women in my life, I made some changes. The following was my wake up call. If you're smart you'll let it be yours too. I sometimes chew my fingernails when I am stressed out. I don't even notice I'm doing it. I chew until there is no nail left and make my fingers look like shit. Women noticed my messed up fingers. It became a turn off to them.

You are a complete dumbass if you think women don't notice shit like this. Let me give you an example in case you're doubting me about this. I was having sex with a woman, and her toe nails scratched me up on my leg pretty good. I'm smart enough that I knew if I wanted to continue having sex, my best bet was to let it slide without saying anything. You should never ruin the mood once you've finally convinced a woman to have sex with you. That's just stupid.

Wait until well after you've gotten your fill of her before you bring anything up that might remotely ruin the mood. Later on that night, I casually asked her if she enjoyed getting pedicures. She said she did love to get her toes done, but hadn't gone for a pedicure in a while. Of course I already knew that because the monster claws on her feet had dug the shit out of me. But you see, I was hoping to subtly get her thinking about making a pedicure appointment in the near future. If she went to the salon and took care of her nasty feet, I would avoid getting more brutal scratches on my shins from her nasty, scraggly toenails.

I was feeling pretty slick about my little plan until she opened her mouth and said, "You know you should really do something with your ragged cuticles and fingernails. You should stop chewing on your nails like that. It's not exactly sexy you know." I never told her I chewed my fingernails. I didn't need to. Just like I already knew she wasn't getting regular pedicures, she had noticed my nasty looking hands. She knew I was complaining about her toes, and came right back at me with the fingernail comments. In all fairness, she was well within her right to do so.

If you want to have a woman that has perfect fingernails and toenails, yours sure as hell better have perfect fingernails and toes as well. Don't expect her to be perfectly groomed if your own grooming habits are less than stellar. This is what I like to call baiting the hook for the fish you want to catch. If you wanted to catch a big beautiful fish, you wouldn't bait the hook with an ugly, old, dried-up and dead worm. If you want to attract only the best, you must offer only the best.

Unless you're planning on shelling out some major cash for a high-end whore, odds are, if your hygiene sucks, so will that of the women you attract. Don't go fishing for large-mouth bass with goldfish flakes. It won't work. Ever!

Still don't believe me? Here's another example. I was caught chewing my fingernails by a different woman I was regularly having sex with. One afternoon while she and I were hanging out, I chewed a little too much, and my index finger started to bleed. She saw me bleeding, stood up, rushed off to the bathroom, and came back with a band aid in her hand.

I said, "Oh, it'll be fine. I don't need that." She laughed and proceeded to correct me by saying, "That bloody finger is not going to be inside me. Don't even think about it. It's disgusting. Put the fucking band aid on, and use the other hand tonight if you want to touch this pussy."

Guys, I cannot emphasize enough how important it is to keep your hands clean and your nails neat. It's a big deal to women. It can mean the difference between a hot romp between the sheets and a set of rolled eyes, and yet another night alone. Here's one final example for you to think about. Never underestimate the importance of what I'm telling you here. Being clean makes it easier to get laid. Being dirty guarantees you're not going to get laid. I really want to drive home just how critically important this is.

A friend of mine was employed as a car mechanic. He was always talking about how he couldn't understand why he was such a failure when it came to picking up women. This guy hadn't been laid in over six months. Six fucking months! My dick hurts just thinking about a dry spell that long. Understandably, this guy was really starting to get desperate.

He tried everything he could think of. New clothes, haircut, new shoes, yet he still had no luck whatsoever. Near the end of yet another night of striking out with every single woman in sight, a drunk woman told him rudely, "You're not touching me with those filthy hands!" Though he had showered after work before he hit the bar, his hands still had paint splotches on them from the car he painted earlier in the day. In fact, his hands were stained with a rainbow of colors from all of the cars he'd painted at work during the entire last week.

This loud, bitchy, drunk woman actually did my friend a huge favor that night, even though he may not have realized it at the time. He complained about this woman's mouthy attitude and rude comment. He should have probably thanked her for cluing him in to the issue. Now he knew why he couldn't get the time of day when he tried to hit on women. At least he should have. This guy was so thick headed he still didn't understand what the big fucking deal was. He asked me, "Shouldn't a woman just be glad that I've got a damn job?"

After I resisted the urge to punch him in the gut, I told him why he was losing out with the ladies month after month. In case you're still a bit lost as well, I will explain it to you also my friend. A lot of men don't understand that women are completely turned off by any part of a man's body being dirty. A quick rinse in the shower and spritz or two of some cheap cologne isn't going to cut it. If his hands or any other body part appears unclean, he will not get laid. No exceptions! I don't care if it's your damn elbow that's got crud on it. Here's why it's such a turn off for her.

Think back to that lame and awkward sex education class your gym teacher made you sit through in middle school. Think about the one single most basic and fundamental fact of life we learned all those years ago. In order for you to get laid, a woman has to literally allow you to place part of your body inside of hers. If you don't know what I'm talking about as far as how a penis and vagina fit together, you need a whole different book dude. Walk on over to the library and read a damn science book already. You've got way bigger problems than my book can help you with.

If your hands or other body part looks filthy, she will assume your dick is too. Got it now? Dirty hands equal a dirty dick as far as she is concerned. It's impossible to turn a woman on who thinks you are dirty. You are not getting laid if you're not clean. Think of it this way, would you put some woman's hand in your month if she just picked up dog shit off the floor with it?

I'm sure some of you are saying, "If she is sexy and she'd fuck me, then HELL YEAH!" Let me go ahead and put it another way so some of you gear heads can understand. Would you mix dirt and gasoline in a gas can? If you did happen to do so, would you then proceed to put that in your classic hot rod? Hell no, that would be stupid as shit. Well, she's the hot rod, her pussy is her motor, and your dick is what makes that motor hum. Always offer the equivalent of premium fuel if you get my drift. Her engine will purr like a happy pussy cat, and your own motor will get to enjoy the smooth ride.

Clothing appearance matters as well. I have discussed this with many of my friends over the years. They say my clothes are terrible. I think they say that mainly because they spend two to three times more money on their clothing than I do. It is true, you have to be willing to spend some money on clothes. That doesn't mean you can't look nice for the ladies even if you're on a budget. I am living proof. It doesn't matter if your clothes are from Sears or a custom tailor downtown, if you treat them right, you will look sharp.

If your twenty-five hundred dollar Armani suit looks like you pulled it out of the dirty clothes basket, you're not going to impress anyone. You would be better off wearing a ten dollar thrift store suit that's clean and professionally pressed. You can look like a slob no matter what you're wearing if you don't take the time properly care for your clothing. Likewise, you can look great in just about anything if it fits, and it's clean and pressed.

You have to iron your pants and shirts. If you don't know how to iron either learn or take your things to the cleaners and have them do it. Simply ironing your shirt and pants can drastically improve your appearance compared to the next guy.

Wear nice shoes when you are going out. Polish them frequently, and make sure you replace your laces as needed. Don't go around with scuffed up shoes and frayed shoelaces and expect to be scoring with women. I have had women compliment me on my shoes in bars. This isn't because they cost hundreds of dollars or had some designers name stamped on the insole. It was because my shoes are always shined and buffed and well taken care of. Don't be lazy. Invest a few minutes and shine your damn shoes so you look like a man and not a little boy who just ran through a pile of dirt on the playground.

So now you know three of the most important items to spend your time and money keeping in tip top shape. Your hands and fingernails, your clothing, and your shoes. Keep your hands clean. Keep your fingernails clean, trimmed, and manicured. Keep your clothing clean and pressed. Keep your shoes polished and scuff free. Women will look at your fingernails and shoes and attempt to determine how much money you make. We all know women are into guys with money. If you look like you're a big fish raking in major amounts of cash, she will think you are less of a predator, and will feel more comfortable around you. Remember, your first impression is made before you even say a word.

If you've already got your nails, clothes, and shoes in tip-top shape, I've got another appearance issue that almost every guy screws up. Your wallet. It doesn't matter if you have thousands of dollars in it. If it's beat all to hell and falling apart at the seams, you look like a chump. Wallets are inexpensive, and there's no reason not to have an attractive leather wallet that you are not embarrassed to pull out when it's time to pay your tab.

You've also got to wear the right clothes to the right place. Make sure you go only to bars and clubs for which you are dressed appropriately. If you go to a country and western bar dressed like you just got out of a business meeting, you'll stand out and get attention. I'm not talking about good attention.

Nobody wears a three-piece suit to a country bar. If the other dudes are all wearing Wranglers and button-up western shirts, you are going to look like an asshole in a suit. Women who go to a country bar want to line dance and two step with a man who's into country music like they are. That's why they have chosen to visit that particular venue.

I'm not saying you won't get attention. I just highly doubt the attention you get is going to get you laid. You're more likely to get laughed at. As with all the scenarios I cover in this book, feel free to test this out for yourself. If I were you, I'd rather take advantage of the experiences of those who came before me. Don't repeat history. Especially when you already know that history predicts your actions will result in a dismal failure.

Here's another example for you to learn from. Yet again, you can benefit from another guy's misfortune this way. My friend told me all about his recent experience in a country bar.

After I got done laughing at him, I decided to share his stupidity with all of you as a stellar illustration of how this plays out in the real world.

My buddy went to a country dance bar wearing shorts. Of course every other damn dude in the place was wearing skin tight Wrangler blue jeans, and here was my friend looking like an idiot in a pair of plaid golf shorts and matching polo shirt. He stuck out like a sore thumb from the rest of the guys in the crowd. They were all wearing cowboy boots, blue jeans and a western style button up shirt. There was no way he could blend in even a little bit. He dressed in this odd way on purpose. He honestly believed this would give him an advantage over all of the other guys and get him laid.

He thought it would gain him massive attention from all the women. In fact, it was very much the opposite reaction he received. Women went out of their way to ignore him, because they were not there to meet someone that looked as if they just strolled off the damn golf course. They probably assumed he dated women with trust funds and names like Buffy or Caroline.

The women at this bar wanted to meet, dance with, and get to know a guy they could relate to. A man who shared their interest in country music and line dancing. When you think of country music, do you think of golf? Hell no! That's why my friend's plan was bound to fail before he even set foot inside the place.

It's not because the bar was short on prospects either. There were plenty of good looking women there. However, my friend couldn't get the time of day from any of them. He stood out from the crowd dramatically, and he couldn't even strike up a conversation. It is okay to stand out slightly. I'm not saying you have to look like a carbon copy of the model on a billboard advertising the club. Be yourself. Be unique. Just don't overdo it to the point women think you're weird and want nothing to do with you.

Always keep your appearance appropriate for the environment you're going to be in. Go to a country bar wearing jeans, boots or nice shoes, and a shirt with a collar. Go to a dance club with nice shoes and pretty much anything you can move in. Obviously, don't go to a dance club if you aren't going to dance. For some reason, some guys don't understand that a dance bar is for dancing. It's not a complex concept. Use your brain!

I am always shocked by the number of men who go to a dance bar, and then just sit there and never ask any of the women to dance. Why the fuck are you at a dance club? If you hate to dance, get the hell out of the dance club. The women who are there like to dance and you will not win any points by sitting on your ass all night refusing to hit the dance floor.

When you meet a woman and there is music and a dance floor, odds are high she is going to want to dance. I went to a New Year's Eve party a couple of years back, and there was a large dance floor. I didn't know it was going to be a dance party, but it turned out that was the situation once I arrived. It definitely worked to my advantage. I met many women that night. Basically I started out the conversation with introductions and then just walked them straight out onto the dance floor. Honestly, I lost count of how many women kissed me that night. If I had just sat around instead of dancing, I wouldn't have gotten a single kiss.

Let's review what we've covered in this chapter. If you are not dressed properly, you'll look like a joke at best. At worst, you'll look like someone that is trying too hard, and is desperate to have sex. Think about where you are headed when you decide what to wear. Also realize women and their friends will be judging you based on your appearance. It's a fact.

As I've already explained to you in the earlier chapters, women seldom go out by themselves to a bar or club. So, you'll have to impress the woman you want to get into bed, as well as the friend or group of friends she's with. The woman you want to date will ask her friends what they think of you. If her friend thinks you look like shit, they will tell her exactly what they're thinking. Women value what their friends think. If the friend tells her you aren't attractive, you're done. Game over.

Sometimes there will even be another dude evaluating you. If the woman you want to date is out with another couple, it's usually her friend and her friend's boyfriend or husband. Don't think having a guy in the mix will help you out. It won't. To the other dude, you are competition. Even though you aren't after his girlfriend, he is still going to size you up as competition. Don't make the mistake of thinking he's on your side. He doesn't know you from Adam, and he's not going to be your wing man or help you get a piece of ass. If you look like shit, he'll happily point it out to the girl you're trying to hook up with. Don't make it easy for him to ruin your chances of getting laid.

Let's talk about another strategy some guys try that backfires on them every time. The only thing worse than underdressing for your environment is overdressing for it. If you overdress for any situation, you'll look desperate. I was out with a friend of mine who loves to wear high-priced dress shirts, shoes, and pants when we go out. It really doesn't matter where we go, he wears them regardless. He is a body builder and a very attractive man. When we go out to most clubs, he does very well with women. From time to time though, he strikes out because of his refusal to adjust his style of dress to the appropriate situation.

We went to a sports bar one night, and he started a conversation with a gorgeous woman. After several drinks, he excused himself to use the bathroom. At that point, the woman he had been flirting with quite bluntly asked me, "Why is he dressed like that? He looks like a rich dumbass." Then she stood up and walked away.

He came back from the bathroom and wondered where the hell she went. All I could do was laugh and give him shit for not dressing for the situation. It was a sports bar not a downtown martini bar. It's not impressive to wear fancy clothes to a sports bar. It just makes you look like a pretentious asshole.

Chapter 5 – Preparing for Introductions

Preparing to initiate a conversation with a stranger can be tough. It's intimidating and takes a lot of self-confidence. Men and women alike have difficulty striking up conversations with members of the opposite sex. The simple truth is, you have to get over your fear and make it second nature. There are some interesting facts about body language I can share to make it easier for you. Keep an eye out for key body language clues from the woman you want to meet. Knowing what to watch for will go a long ways towards building your confidence and improving your results when you approach women for the first time.

For example, you need to watch for openings. I'm always on the lookout for more than one quick glance in my direction from a woman I'm interested in. If I notice her looking at me just once, this could mean she has something in her eye. It could mean she is looking at the guy right behind me. I don't have enough information yet to know for sure if she's into me or not. One glance, or even one stare from a woman looking in your direction is not enough of a signal to go by. Don't ever get cocky and assume she's into you based on one single look in your direction. While I always notice a first glance, I don't totally rely on it as a clue that it's a great time to approach her and strike up a conversation.

Before you decide to go any further, you need to observe her and see if you pick up more hints that she's into you. Whatever you do though, don't be creepy about it. Don't stare at her. Look around the room in general, but also keep an eye out for more glances from the woman that are cast in your direction. If you make eye contact and it lasts for more than a second, take it as a good sign. Go talk to her. If eye contact doesn't last, she may be shy. Failure to make eye contact could also indicate she is already in a relationship with a man. I have noticed married women who are not wearing their wedding rings tend to do this. For any number of reasons, they are feeling uncomfortable as they consider being unfaithful to their husband.

Regardless, you haven't talked with her yet, so you have to look at her body language to figure out what she's thinking and if you should approach her. This reduces the chance of being shot down because you are not simply guessing if she may be interested. There are lots of little body language signs you can look for.

If her arms are down, it signals warmth and openness. Crossed arms are the equivalent of a, "closed for business" sign hanging in a storefront window. Avoid approaching any woman who has her arms crossed. Look instead for signals that she is interested in meeting you. She should be smiling. In the best possible case scenario, she will be smiling and posing in an open stance as she consistently gazes in your direction.

Now I don't want you to mistake any of these behaviors as a sure thing. I have attempted to initiate conversations with women that displayed all of the ideal indicators prior to making my first approach, and it meant nothing. Body language is just one of many clues you should count on using to accurately gauge if a woman is interested in you.

Body language signals are a small piece of the big picture. It is not the golden ticket that guarantees you a successful conversation. Like anything else, body language at its best is nothing more than a hint that you possibly have a chance with her. Don't let this lack of a guarantee make you feel nervous though. If the potential for getting shot down bothers you, you need to go up to bat more. Practice. Then get out and practice some more.

Once you start the conversation, don't hesitate to bail if things aren't going well. If you pay attention to her body language and really listen to her, you'll know right away if she's at all interested. As I have said before and will continue to say, "Watch for the easy out." When a woman doesn't give you the opportunity to talk to her, don't stalk her. Don't waste your time and try and convince her she should like you. Have a little pride and walk away. Just take it as your sign that she isn't interested and move on. However, sometimes the easy out can be hard to recognize.

I met a woman and we danced for hours. I wanted to go further. I leaned in to kiss her, and she turned away from me. I didn't push any harder that night, but I thought there may be an opportunity later. So, I got her number and we spoke on the phone and sent several text messages back and forth. Keep in mind, she called and texted me just as much as I did her. She never actually said any words I'd categorize as, "You have no fucking shot." Eventually, she stopped contacting me, and so I stopped contacting her. I never really knew what happened, but I just kind of forgot about it after a few days had went by.

A few weeks later, I was out, and a couple of our mutual friends told me she thought I was stalking her. I laughed and then deleted her number from my phone. Long story short, when I tried to kiss her, and she turned away, I should've taken that as my easy out and moved on. I missed it, and I ended up making her uncomfortable and wasting my time on a women I was never going to get into bed.

Have you ever seen a scary movie where a man is following a woman as she runs away? Do you really want to be that guy chasing a screaming woman through the forest trying to catch her? Think of it this way. Do you want your face associated with every scary movie she's ever seen? Don't be a dick. Take the easy out and move on at the first obvious sign she's not interested. She will not change her mind down the road. Cut your losses and move on.

Chapter 6 – Body Language Speaks for You

Body language speaks volumes. It communicates for you without a single word coming out of your mouth. It is very important to remember when a woman is checking you out or speaking with you for the first time, she may not consciously realize it, but she is sizing you up. For that matter, you may not notice either unless you've had a lot of practice.

So what is a woman's purpose when she is checking you out? When you are checking a woman out, you're thinking about how hot she'll be in bed. You're thinking you'd love to touch those round perky tits. I hate to disappoint you, but it's not the same with her. She is observing you, and attempting to determine if you are a predator or someone she can potentially trust and let into her body.

It's not difficult to figure out what your body language should be. Your goal should be to look like you're not intimidating or a threat for her. Stand or sit without crossing your arms. If your arms are crossed, it makes you look irritated and defensive. If you have decent teeth and don't look like you got hit by a hockey puck, than smile. Damn you, Smile!

Not smiling makes you look like you don't want to be there with her and you're not interested in whatever she is talking about. She will take this to mean you are not interested in her, and you will be rejected. Hell, half the time I am not even listening to whatever lame bullshit she is rambling on about. I still smile and nod like her story about her grandma, her cat or whatever other boring fucking nonsense she's going on and on about is the most fascinating thing I've heard in weeks.

The other point I want to make about your body language is this one. When you smile, she will be more inclined to smile back at you. If you meet a woman for the first time, smile. If she smiles back and makes eye contact, that is a good opening for you. She's probably interested in you. Remember, if a woman likes her smile, she wants men to notice it. If she doesn't smile back, don't bother approaching her and trying to hit it off.

Well, at least don't try right then. The timing isn't right. Wait a little while, and see if she starts showing more warm and open body language signaling as the evening progresses. If she does, then go and talk with her. If she doesn't ever warm up, she doesn't want to be there and just wants to be left alone. Or, she's just not interested, and you need deal with that reality and move on.

Another form of body language you should make sure you monitor yourself for is your posture. I have terrible posture. I have to constantly remind myself to sit up when seated, and push my chest out and walk with a very confident pose. I have had women not be interested in me just because I didn't look confident when I was talking with them.

The reason I didn't appear confident in these instances is solely because of how poor my posture was. One woman actually told me, "You don't look secure in yourself." I asked why, and she replied, "You just don't." I honestly don't think she knew why I didn't look confident. But after a little reflection on my part, I figured out it was my posture that had given her this idea about me.

Women want a man who looks confident. You don't necessarily need to be confident, but at least do your best to look like you are. Consider yourself a trophy that every woman would want on her arm. If you are confident, warm, and present a shit load of positive body language, she'll want you, and also present you to her friends willingly.

Remember, if it doesn't work out with the woman you are currently with, you may have a shot at her friends. You want to impress them and make them want to fuck your brains out. If you do, the woman you are currently with will think you are a big trophy, and hopefully fuck your eyes out that much more often.

Here's another way to think of it. If everyone knew you were fucking a supermodel, would your friends be jealous of you? Hell yes they would! They may even try to get you out of the picture so they could fuck her. Women aren't always as aggressive as men are. But, if given the opportunity to take you as a trophy, especially if she's hotter than the woman you are currently sleeping with, you want to allow the opportunity to happen.

When a woman is proud of you and considers you her trophy, she will show you off. She'll stand behind you and show her friends what kind of man she can really get. If you fail to meet her expectations of what type of man she could potentially attract, she'll stand behind you in shame. If you don't meet her expectations, she'll keep looking.

You want her to show you off. It gives you the opportunity to meet more hot women without even trying. The women that don't show you off may be really into you but make you do stupid things. I had a friend that had a very dirty blue collar job. His wife made him dress in business suits and speak professionally whenever they were around other people. She did that so she could be proud of what she did to improve his looks. Her self-esteem was not at a level that she could date someone with the look she desired, so she dressed my friend up to look like she could.

When it comes to using body language and presenting yourself as the trophy, you aren't doing it for yourself. You are doing it for her self-esteem. You are a man. Don't be a pussy, and keep yourself presented in an open, attractive, warm and inviting way. This will help her self-esteem. If you have more or less self-esteem then she does, that'll drive her away. Be confident, and help her to be confident in you. Let me put it this way. Water finds its own level. This means you need to find out what level her current self-esteem is and match it. If you can't match it, move on and find a woman that you can match.

Chapter 7 – Starting and Building a Conversation

So, how do you start a conversation with a woman? You already know you need to present warm positive body language and appear confident. Remember, you don't need to actually be confident, you just need to look like you are. You've watched your targets body language and posture, and you're prepared to head on over and start a conversation with her. You know it might be a good conversation, or you might get shot down in flames in less than a millisecond. Just stop worrying about it and go over and talk to her.

I like the phrase, "If you never go up to bat, you'll never hit a home run." Go up to bat, and start the conversation by quickly figuring out a subject she'll want to talk about. For example, if she has well groomed fancy fingernails, she didn't spend all that time on them not to get noticed. So, notice them. Tell her what you like about them. If you don't like them, lie. Who the hell cares? Just get her talking to you.

If she's wearing a lot of jewelry, notice it. Some women dress unusually or in bright colors in an attempt to stand out and be noticed by others. She wants to be noticed, so notice her! Basically, just start the conversation with something she will want to talk about. Generally speaking, women love to talk about themselves. Let them.

Keep your conversation all about her, and all about what she likes. If she asks you questions, keep the answers short and turn the conversation back around to her. Act like she's the most fascinating human being you've ever met in your entire life. Even if talking with her is more boring than watching paint dry, don't let it show in your body language or facial expressions unless you want to blow it.

As the conversation progresses, you'll be able to figure out what she spends her time and money on. If you know anything about the topic, take advantage of that. Talk with her about her favorite subject. It might be her kids or pets. It could be her job, or something totally off the wall like pottery or dog shows. If you can't figure out what she's excited about in life, there are ways you can get a clue. Look for a key chain or a locket around her neck. They will typically have pictures in them. Ask her about it, and she'll probably happily babble on for as long as you can stand to listen.

If you are at a bar, another good topic to talk about is what she's drinking. I met a woman who wasn't wearing any jewelry, and I couldn't initially determine what topic to discuss with her. However I know there is always a clue, so I kept looking for an idea. She was drinking a glass of red wine. So, I asked her about it. That started a long very detailed conversation about the different types of wines that she likes, and the vacations she's taken to different regions of the world famous for winemaking.

We didn't have sex that night, but I met up with her about a week later, and she was all over me. We didn't have sex that second night either. I actually went out with her four times before we had sex the first time. But when we did, she fucked the hell out of me. I was sore for two days afterwards! It was certainly more than worth the wait.

As you begin talking to more and more women, you should focus on learning to really tune in and pay attention. Take the time to listen to her. You really don't need to say much. Listen to her, and she'll teach you something that will most likely be useful later on down the road. It may be something you could care less about, but who the hell cares.

She cares about it. And, if you pay attention, you can use the information you learned in the conversation with a different woman in the future.

I've run into many women that like to sew. I hate sewing. The very thought of it makes me cringe. But I know how to talk about it. There is a sewing machine called a Serger. It's a very expensive high end sewing machine. So, I ask any woman I'm talking to about sewing if she has a Serger.

If she has one, she won't shut up about it, and all I have to do is sit there and listen. I've already scored big points in her mind for knowing about a topic that's important to her. Build common ground with her. Keep her interested in whatever you are talking about. It doesn't really matter if you are. Don't talk about yourself. Don't think about yourself. It's not about you right now. It's all about her. Remember that, and you will do just fine.

There are a lot of various approaches that guys can take when first meeting a woman. Some men start with a simple hello and a smile or a basic, "What's your name?" While others get a bit more creative and ask the lady for directions to her pants.

While most players nowadays will agree that the "pickup line" is a notion that's run its course, making her laugh is still effective and always will be. Just make sure it isn't you that she is laughing at. There isn't a person in the world who doesn't like to laugh. A lot of the most successful relationships are full of laughs, jokes and smiles. If you want to get to know her because you are looking at her for a possible long-term relationship, or if you just want to find out if she is as flexible as she looks, making her laugh is always a great start.

Why is making her laugh the key to unlocking the zipper on her skirt? It's all in our basic human nature. The main personality trait anyone looks for in another person is their ability to make them feel better than they already do. Of course there are a lot of different factors that play into whether or not a certain person can make you happy. The way they look, the way that they treat other people, their ideals and the values they hold, and of course how often they like to make the mattress shake all matter when deciding if being around that person will make you feel happy.

If you are able to get her to smile and laugh the first time the two of you meet, then she will automatically believe that you have a good chance of giving her the good feelings she looks for from the man in her life. Whether or not you can actually make her happy is a different story, but if you make her laugh she will at least consider it as a good possibility.

What's the best way to make her laugh? That really depends on the woman. To make her laugh you will need to be able to read into her personality before you approach her. Yes, you have to judge the book by its cover. This is where being at least somewhat compatible gives you the advantage. If you share the same sense of humor, it's easy to just be yourself and make her laugh. But don't worry, even if you're not compatible, you can still get her laughing. You'll just need to solve the mystery and find out what makes her laugh.

Some girls like dry humor while others prefer sarcasm or goofiness. The best way to get her laughing and to really find out what tickles her funny bone is to start off with a light tease. Tell her she must have had a rough night because her hair is a mess, or ask her if you can get her a glass of water because she seems to be swaying. If she gives you the awkward eye, back off for a second and introduce yourself. Then work your way up until you find out what really puts a smile on her face.

Once you have her laughing and smiling you can really take the night anywhere you want it to go. You can grab her cell number and meet up later that week, or go big and see if you can get her to laugh her panties right off of her and onto your bedroom floor. The possibilities are endless.

So how do you know if she's into you after the two of you start talking? First let's touch on one negative signal to look out for. There is one warning sign that the conversation is not going well that you'll probably think is an indicator she's actually really into you. You can be totally caught off guard if you don't know to watch out for it. Some women pretend to be interested in you for some odd reason. Don't waste your time trying to figure it out. If she starts asking a lot of questions, take that as a huge warning sign. Questions like, "What is that?" or, "I've never heard of that, can you tell me about it?" are not good. You may think she is interested in you because she's asking you questions. She's not. She is either interested in your friend, or she has a boyfriend or husband, and she's too chicken to cheat on them. Regardless, ditch the bitch and move to the next one.

If you catch yourself talking about yourself, change the topic. You are dull. Nobody cares about you. To get the woman naked, she has to be curious about you. If she barely knows your name after the first time you have sex with her, you're doing a good job. You should shoot for over seventy percent of all your conversations consisting of her speaking about herself.

I met one woman who had dated her boyfriend for four years. I asked her what he did for a living. She had no idea. All she knew is that he travelled all the time, so she only saw him two or three times a month. He was the person who ended the relationship. I asked her if she wanted him to come back to her. She said, "He had his chance." Let me translate this for you. This really means, "Yes. I'd take him back in a second, and I won't even care about why he dumped me." Keeping yourself a bit of a mystery is always something to strive for.

If the conversation is going well, don't be afraid to touch her. For example, if you have been listening to a woman talk for several minutes about her jewelry, touch the piece of jewelry she seems to like the most. If she doesn't seem to care that you are touching her, and you need to be careful here, touch another piece of jewelry. Just don't be too aggressive or you'll piss her off.

Although, as with most things in life, there are exceptions to the rule. My friend Joe is extremely aggressive when he speaks with women. He will start a conversation with a woman that has fake boobs just so he could ask her about them. After discussing her boobs, he'd reach out and touch them. He'd even ask about her nipple size and if she likes her nipples bitten. I've seen him have this conversation with many women. Several got pissed off and told him to fuck off. Others were into the discussion and liked him touching their tits. She wanted men to notice them. I normally don't recommend being this aggressive, but it worked for Joe from time to time. Bottom line, if you get the feeling her tits are her favorite accessory, run with it. Never pass up a chance to talk about titties.

Chapter 8 – Buying a Woman Drinks

So maybe you have heard the phrase, "The more she drinks the less she thinks." Or perhaps you've heard, "The only thing better than alcohol is more alcohol." Well, I am here to tell you that buying a drink for a woman at the bar is one of both the oldest, and the most annoying traditions around. Who the hell came up with this dumb ass idea? "Gee, I think I'll spend my hard-earned money on a stranger who may not even care to say hello." Talk about dumb or dumber. No, no, no! It's a terrible plan that will never pay off in the way you think it will.

Simply put, don't be a sucker and hand your paycheck over to some broad you don't know shit about. Don't buy a woman drinks. If you think that buying her drinks is going to get you laid, it won't. The only chance you have is if she is by herself and you get her totally hammered. Then, and only then, will buying her drinks probably get your dick wet. The reason it works in this instance is simply because, if she is there by herself, she doesn't have someone to go out with. She's lonely, and women absolutely hate to be lonely.

Now don't make the mistake of assuming she's single or not dating anyone. That's not necessarily the case. Take the situation for what it is and nothing more. It just means she didn't have someone to pal around with at that moment.

Maybe she had a fight with her boyfriend. Maybe her husband cheated on her. Maybe she's just tired of hanging out by herself every night. It doesn't matter what the reason is, because they all raise the chances of getting a piece of ass from her. She has already allowed herself to be alone in a bar. She already let some random guy she just met get her drunk. Chances are high this is a woman who will probably not see it as much of a stretch to allow herself to have sex with a stranger. Lucky you. If you play your cards right, you're going to score tonight.

Just don't be dumb enough to think you are the only guy she's given a wet dick to within a few hours of their first meeting. Also, whenever a woman is alone, be suspicious. Here's what I mean by this. I met a woman in a bar. Not only was she hot as hell, she was sitting there on a bar stool all by herself. I went over and started talking with her. Much to my delight, the conversation quickly started to get dirty. Really dirty.

I am a pretty straight forward guy. Being such, I didn't hesitate to flat out ask her, "Are you going to take me home tonight?" She said, "More than likely." I was happy with that, and my dick was already starting to twitch. But, as well as being a straight shooter, I'm also a very curious type of person. So, next I asked her what she did for a living.

Without hesitation she told me she worked at one of the local topless joints. She was a stripper. I should have guessed it. Although she was on the chunky side for a stripper, her behavior was just a little too forward for your average girl. So there you have it. She was a damn stripper. Hey, I don't discriminate. It is a job after all. I figured, who am I to judge? After all, strippers are flexible as hell, and those girls really know how to move their hips. This could turn out to be a night I would not soon forget.

I said, "You must get hit on by guys every night. Do you ever take your customers home and have sex with them?" She answered, "Oh yeah. Almost every night. I love sex. I'm a very sexual person." The gears in my head started spinning, and I began to plug in a few numbers. The idea of fucking this chic suddenly got a lot less appealing.

You do the math gentlemen. Depending on how long this girl had been taking her clothes off for a living, she could have been with 100 men or even more. Red flags were going off for me by then. So, I had to ask even though I normally don't care, "How many men have you slept with then? Do you even know?" She told me, "Somewhere between 250 and 350. Oh, and by the way, I have herpes. Is that going to be a problem for you?" It was, and I got the hell away from that bitch as quickly as possible. There is nothing less appealing then a slut with herpes. What the hell was she thinking?

If you think buying a woman drinks is going to impress her, it doesn't. Save your money. I dated a woman that other men also found extremely attractive. They would send drinks to her even though I was sitting at the table with her. She would laugh at how men spent money sending her drinks but didn't even stop by and talk to her, not that she wanted them to. If they did stop by, she'd just blow them off and laugh about it. In her eyes, a man sending her a drink was a loser, and didn't have the confidence or skill to have a conversation with her. He had to use sending drinks as his only tool to meet women. Basically, she felt these drink-buying men were just that: tools.

Now these days, there are drugs some men put in drinks to drug a woman and then sleep with them. Therefore, more and more women are getting suspicious if a man buys a drink and gives it to her. I've known several women that won't accept the drink if you hand it to her. It has to come from the bartender or wait staff. This can be a good thing and a bad thing. If she has been raped, she'll probably have issues. If you really like her, you'll need to be very patient and understanding. If she hasn't been raped, she is cautious and may still have issues, just different issues. Regardless, she is probably isn't the type of woman you are going to score with on that first night. It will probably take at least a few dates.

Some women dress sexy so men will foolishly buy drinks for them. Their goal isn't to get laid, but to improve their own self-worth by having men give them free drinks. I met this cute little brunette, not at a bar. I asked her out and even attempted to coax her to going to a bar with me by offering to buy the drinks for her. She floored me by what she said. She said, "If I want free drinks, I'll dress slutty and go to the bar." Needless to say, we didn't go out. I got shot down. I count this as a blessing though. She obviously has a habit of dressing slutty just to get free drinks!

Don't think married women won't play this game. Married women are often much worse than single women. It's really about self-worth to them. If single guys hit on them, whether or not she admits she is married, it makes her feel better about herself. I was in a bar and my friend was talking to an attractive single woman. So, I took one for the team and talked with her friend to keep her busy. She was married, and I wasn't really interested in her anyway. Regardless, I noticed her drink was empty. So, she gives me this really pouty look and says, "I know, and my purse is all the way over there!" She was pointing at the other side of the bar. I just replied, "Oh that must suck. I'm going to go buy myself another beer. I'll be right back." When I got back, ironically, she had a new drink.

Groups of married women can be even worse than that. One night, I saw a group of married women walk in and take off their rings. They spent the night seeing who could get the most drinks bought for them. That way their husbands did not see a big amount of money removed from the checking account or added to the credit card. The husbands then foolishly thought she must have not had much to drink at the bar. In reality, she was hanging on other men all night to get hammered for free.

Don't think this is limited to free drinks either. Women in a committed relationship will do a lot to hide activity from showing up on the bank statements or credit account statements. Years back I read a story in the newspaper about this. The police set up a sting to see who was buying drugs from a local dealer. Many housewives came in and exchanged drugs for sex so it wouldn't be discovered by their partner that they had a big money drug habit.

Chapter 9 – Handling Rejection

There are two types of men. Those that get rejected by women and hold it personally, and those that get rejected and don't hold it personally. The men that get rejected and are offended will only score on undesirable women with low self-esteem. He might date her for a while, feel better about himself, and attempt to move himself up to the next level. He'll then date someone who is not as undesirable as the last women and repeat the process. This is called, "date someone until your self-esteem gets healthier." The men that don't get offended and handle the rejection the right way will score, and score a lot and skip the years working up the ladder.

When you meet a woman for the first time, unless you can read minds, you don't really know what she's thinking. You can read her body language and attempt to interpret what she's saying to get a feel, but that isn't always accurate. Always leave her an "easy out" so she can reject you easily. I know this may sound odd, but because you can't read minds, give her an opportunity to reject you without making it difficult for her. If you do, when you see her again, it won't feel weird. I've been rejected by women and I gave them an easy out. It can work in your benefit. I met a woman in a bar and talked with her. I gave her an "easy out" and she took it. Later, I saw her and talked with her again. This time, I asked her who she thought I would do well with. She introduced me to her very cute friend who I danced with and made out with the rest of the night. I didn't sleep with her that night. She made me wait until the next day. I met another woman a different night who took the "easy out" and then proceeded to give me ideas on who I should talk to next. She even gave me ideas on how I should start the conversation with the woman.

Sometimes, if you give her an "easy out", it improves her opinion of you. Women are very competitive. If you take the rejection and really don't care or let it offend you, she may think you don't rate her very high. Sometimes, that can work in your favor. If her own self-confidence is insulted because her rejection didn't really bother you, she may take a second look at you. It all really depends on how you handle the rejection.

Her self-esteem and her self-confidence are not up to you to change. It is her emotional health at the time. There is a phrase I like to use when I talk about this. "Water finds its own level." Because you can't read minds, you don't know how she's feeling. But, if you are a two and she's a ten, and you're hitting on her when her confidence is low, you might have a chance, albeit a slim chance. But if she is feeling down and you can somehow make her feel better, go for it.

You have to remember, a woman is not a pig you are trying to trap in a pen. If you corner a pig in a pen, it gets frightened. So do women. Remember my buddy Joe? He's the guy that uses a super aggressive approach when he first meets women. I saw him sit next to a woman in a booth and start touching her leg. She didn't tell him to stop, so he grabbed her tits. She couldn't leave the booth because he was blocking her in. She was cornered. She drew back and punched my friend in the face and then kicked him out of the booth. She shouted, "Asshole!" Joe just shrugged his shoulders and said, "I don't know why she's mad!" I called him a dumbass and was shocked he couldn't figure that out on his own.

Often something easy to get is not as desirable as something hard to get. If you could buy a Porsche for the same price as a Toyota, would you? You may be a Toyota, but if you give her an "easy out", you are helping your cause. Strive for the Porsche at the Toyota cost.

There are many types of women, and I could go on and on about that, but you need to watch out for the type of woman that hates the "easy out". She's the type that has the attitude of "I want you to work hard to get me". You can usually tell this type because she'll probably just ask you the question, "I'm not worth your time?" I've even heard, "What's wrong with you? Don't you want to fuck me?" Her self-esteem is based on how much she can make you do for a chance with her. My suggestion for when you encounter this type of woman is to RUN AWAY! Don't worry about her. She'll find some other dumbass that'll play that game with her. Then, when she's built up her self-esteem a bit, she'll dump him horribly and fuck over some other dude, if she doesn't have one already. I was dating a woman who was living with her sister until she could move into her new apartment. Her sister had a long term boyfriend that she'd fight with often. When they fought, her self-esteem went down and she'd go fuck someone else. She'd have sex with him for a week or two while the long term boyfriend and her were fighting, then she'd dump the guy with no explanation. The long term boyfriend didn't know. When they'd fight again, she'd find another dude to screw over until they made up.

Chapter 10 – Dating Do's and Don'ts

If you are just starting to date a woman, you'll need to pay attention. If she says "no" to sex, she may be questioning herself and wondering if you are quality enough to bring into her body. Make sure your hands and nails are clean and manicured. If they are not clean, that is a turn off for her. Your hands are looked at because the fingers may potentially enter her body. She doesn't want dirty grimy fucked up fingers inside her. If you've ever had a prostate exam, you'll appreciate clean hands. Keep your nails trim and clean. If you find a woman that doesn't care about clean presentable hands and fingers, then ask yourself what else has entered her body that hasn't been clean.

Keep yourself clean and smelling good. If you don't smell good, you can't hide it and you won't get laid. Keep your breath smelling fresh. Don't eat garlic if she isn't eating garlic. Your sweat will not be sweet smelling and men sweat all the time. Wear cologne. What works best is to lightly spray yourself twice with cologne. The first spray should be done by spraying in the air and walking through it. The second spray should be done after you get out of the shower on your dick. I know this sounds weird, but this way every time you pee you get a fresh smell and don't smell like a men's room. If she decides to give you a blow job, she won't want you to smell like a toilet.

After you've been dating a woman for a while and having sex with her, you'll start to notice warning signs. Pay attention to them. It is hell recovering from a bad breakup, especially getting dumped when you don't expect it.

There are many warning signs if you know what to watch for. If she starts to question the potential relationship with you, look for delayed times between calls. She is working on getting the next man to dump you for. Remember, women are like monkeys, they won't let go of the branch they have until they can reach another branch. If she starts saying "no" to sex fairly often, she may be thinking there is no need to get close to you or keep you. She is thinking you might just leave if you are not getting sex which would make her life easier. If she changes her hair color or hair style, she is on the market again and trying to get attention. However, changes in appearance may also be to test your reaction. Remember she, in conjunction with her friends, will make the choice if you are to break up. You will just find out about it later.

Sometimes a woman will do things to test you. Watch for these signs. They can give you a lot of insight about her. For example, when a woman changes her appearance suddenly without talking to you first, be careful how you handle this. Start calling her less. This gives her the impression that you are confident and can get another woman of her standard. If she leaves a voicemail or email that sounds negative or angry, wait at least an hour before replying. If you call her back right away yelling and screaming, it tells her a lot about you. Remember, a woman shouldn't know much about you. It's all about her.

If you and your date haven't had sex yet and start messing around, you may get laid or you may not. You need to be prepared for either option. If you think you're going to score and she says something like, "I'm not ready to have sex with you yet", you need to know what to do. I had that happen to me and I handled it totally wrong. I told her that was fine but continued to kiss her and touch her. Eventually, I left and went home. She called the next day and dumped me. The correct way of handling that is to politely stand up, tell her you respect her, and tell her you're going to leave. Be ready to leave gracefully. Sometimes, that will be enough to change her mind, and you'll get lucky. Otherwise, she could be testing you. I was dating a woman going through a divorce but who was currently separated. We went to lunch for the first date and met at a public pool for the second date. She bluntly told me she wasn't ready to have sex with me. I quickly came back with, "That's fine. I understand." After we were done swimming, we went to dinner, had a few drinks and then went to my house and had sex. I teased her later about it. Her reply was, "Well, I changed my mind. I just wanted to set the expectation."

If the two of you get hot and heavy, she may want to see if you go pick up someone else to have sex with. For example, I dated a girl that insisted on testing the man first by getting him all worked up, then telling him "no" to sex. She'd call later to see if he made it home or picked up someone on the way home. She wanted to be the only fish in the pond. By the way, men can play this game too. I have sent out flowers with no name on them to see if she called me and thanked me. If she was waiting for me to say something about it then I knew she has more than one person in the picture. If you leave, you stand a good chance she'll call you the next day. I went on a date and we began to kiss. Kissing turned into clothing being removed. She stopped me and said, "It's getting late." I took this as the "easy out" and agreed by saying, "You're right. I should go." And I kissed her one more time and left. The next day, she called me and wanted to know when I could come and spend the night with her.

As a man, you have to be careful. If you push too hard for sex, in some courts, you could go to jail for rape. I know a man that pushed his date too hard for sex until she finally gave it to him. The next day, she decided she hated it and now he's in prison for rape. There is a very fine line. The court is often left to decide between her word and his word. She will win in a court of law. Don't go there. Walk away. It is best to tease them and have them take your clothing off, because they want you. If you can't get her there, you need to go find someone else to fuck. At the end of the day, it's in her mind and control if you have sex or not.

Sex today is one of the easiest things to get if you're willing to drop your standards. You will see a homeless person going through a dumpster looking for food, but in the alley, he'll have a woman around that he is having sex with.

It's easier to have sex with a woman then to have her tell you she loves you.

If you decide to take a woman out for dinner, watch what you order or you won't get laid later that night. For example, I was dating a woman and the sex was decent. However, after taking her out for a large dinner, the sex sucked. One evening she told me, "When you take me out, I overeat and get too full. And there is no way in hell I am going to get naked when I'm feeling fat. If you want to get laid, don't over feed me." She also noted that some foods make her gassy and nothing is going to happen after that either. Remember, it's all about her and her perception of herself.

Women do have male friends that they aren't currently sleeping with. She may have in the past, but not at the moment. Hell, after she's done with you, she may go sleep with him. You need to watch out for her male friend. Don't get mad when he starts to trash you. You have to play this right. This is someone she talks to and tells all her problems to. Don't attempt to befriend him. He's a dipshit and he's just looking for dirt on you to tell to her. But, you can have some fun with him. Find out what he doesn't like to do and invite him to do those activities. This will keep him away. But, if he does take you up on the offer, enjoy it. He won't. Don't try to fix him up with one of your female friends or attempt to figure out if he's gay or straight. Put your focus where it belongs, on her.

If you decide to have a committed relationship with a woman, you should plan on your male friends acting like assholes. Face it, if you go out and hit on women every weekend with your buddy, your buddy will get used to it. If you meet a woman, date for a while, and decide to go into a committed relationship with her, your buddy won't like it. It is not in his best interest to have you involved with a woman. He wants you acting as his wingman like it was before the woman. You need to watch out for him. I have a friend that liked the sister of a woman I was dating. He'd ask me a ton of questions about the sister and then go up and tell her I told her. Then, the sister would get mad and tell the woman I was dating who in turn got mad at me. So, the lesson I learned was, don't tell your friends a damn thing about the woman you are dating or her family. He'll use it against you to cause problems between her and you. Once she dumps you because of what you told him, you are free to go back to being the wingman every weekend with him.

It's better to wait to tell your friends all this information until after you break up without the help of your asshole friend.

Chapter 11 – Friends with Benefits

Every guy I have ever known that has had the pleasure of having a friend with benefits has enjoyed it, if they played it right. Men want sex. So do women. Many women have as big or bigger sex drive than men do. So, if you find a woman that you can be friends with and still have sex with her, bonus! However, you have to remember that it is not in her best interest to have a sex partner that is in a relationship with another woman. So, if you're fucking someone else, don't tell her. She'll ask about who you're dating. Lie. Make the conversation about her and keep your mouth shut. Friends with benefits follow the same rules as dating, just less hang ups. You still have to remember, it's all about her. Keep the relationship talk down to nearly nothing. It is very easy to cross the line and end up in a relationship with her. Think of it this way. She is giving you sex as a reward for spending time with her. In her eyes, she is killing time until she meets someone. She may even be considering you.

Just like the dating warning signs, keep your eyes open for the big friends with benefits warning sign. If she starts playing the "20 questions game" (you know, the one where she asks you a shit load of questions and demands that you answer them), she is looking for some reason to get out. If you see this warning sign, give her the "easy out". She might take it, but it'll work in your benefit later.

Let's face it. Women can be deceptive. Don't think for a second that because she is your friend that you get to see naked, she won't be deceptive to you. She will lie to you. She'll tell you, "I've never done the friends with benefits thing before." Why would she be deceptive? There are many reasons. She may want you to think she has not been sleeping around with other men. Obviously, some men prefer innocent women. If she hasn't really had sex with a lot of men, she'll lie and tell you all the things she really hasn't had the opportunity to do yet. You can play this back on her though. Just ask her if she wants to do them with you. She probably will, you lucky bastard.

Her self-esteem comes into play here as well. She may not want you to know her self-esteem is lower than what she thinks yours is. Just face the truth. You're filling a need for her with your dick until she finds someone she wants to have a relationship with. If her self-esteem is low, make her feel good about herself. Follow the same rules as though you are dating her. Don't take messages from other women while you are spending time with her. Always do your best to try and make her feel special. She is using you for your dick, but that doesn't mean you need to be a dick in the way you treat her.

So, how do you know when the friends with benefits situation needs to come to an end? You'll know when it's time to run. That is fairly easy to figure out. If she is waiting at home for you and hoping you'll end up with her, she is more than a friend. It is time to end it. If it gets to this point, she'll start to make herself look better in appearance and she'll trash talk other women she knows you'd be attracted to. If you end it, be nice. Don't just tell her, "I don't want to fuck you anymore." That won't be pleasant for anyone. Just tell her you have developed a new respect for her and you think it'll screw up the friendship if you continue to have sex with her. That gives her self-esteem and makes it a positive change.

Chapter 12 – Live Where You Want To Meet Women

When a man finds himself in the midst of a breakup or divorce, he'll typically begin to look around and pay more attention to the women who live and work in his area. All men look at attractive women. That's not exactly groundbreaking information. All guys check out hot women, it's in our genetics.

However, when a guy is in a relationship with a woman, he's usually not aggressively seeking to get laid by women aside from the woman he's currently in a relationship with. There are exceptions to that, of course. But, overall it's pretty much a given that single guys are working much harder to find a woman to have sex with than those who are not.

When the relationship you've been in ends, you start to take notice of the women in the area. Well, what do you do when you live in an area of 50 year olds and you're only 25? Unless you want to have sex with cougars, you won't get laid because there aren't any women your age to hook up with. So, you need to move to an area where you will have an opportunity to meet women you're interested in having sex with.

To scope out a new area, go to restaurants you like to eat at, and check out the single women in the restaurant. Make sure the restaurant specializes in breads and soups. If there are a lot of women your age that you find attractive, that's a good sign. Next, go to the grocery store in the neighborhood you plan to find a house or apartment. If the grocery store doesn't have women you're interested in, you may want to pick a new area to reside. Most people go to grocery stores close to their home. If there are hot women in the store, the odds are good they live close to the store. I lived in an area where the majority of the women were either ten years older than me or ten years younger. I actually liked that because in any one week, I could date one older woman and the next night, a younger woman.

Sometimes, to really scope out an area, you'll need to find yourself a female friend. Make it someone you don't really want to be with, but not an ugly duckling. You want someone who looks good but just is not your type sexually. Let her pick the places to eat, and she will show you where to meet other women. Make sure to always keep it light hearted, and joke around while the two of you are out together. This shows other women you are just friends in case any of them are already checking you out. You don't want to blow an opportunity to get laid because it looks like you're on a date with this chic.

Let her pick out some new clothing for you as well. Most men go out dressed in the same clothing style they were wearing when they met their ex-wife ten years ago. If your clothes were in style ten years ago, they are not in style now. Get some new clothes so you don't look like a suburban soccer dad everywhere you go.

Never underestimate the value of a woman's advice and feedback in your life. I had a close female friend that was great to hang out with. My friend was married, but her husband was frequently out of town for business. They had a couple of kids, but they were grown by the time we started hanging out. She would often get lonely while he was away and I would pick her up and take her out to eat or to a movie once in a while.

I'd always let her pick the place she wanted to eat at and always made sure I treated her like a sister whenever we were out. I even went as far as calling her sis, so the other women would pick up on that in case they might be interested in dating me.

I'd always start out by asking once we arrived at the restaurant, "So how is the hubby doing?" You would be shocked at how this was heard in the cafe. It was fun to watch the faces of those sitting nearby who assumed we were having some sort of illicit affair.

If we didn't head to a restaurant, we usually were at the local shopping mall. I'd let her pick out some new clothing for me. It was a great arrangement for both of us, and I always had a great time when we went out. The best part was, if another good looking women walked into the place we were at, my friend's head turned before mine even did, and I knew exactly where to look. There are major advantages to having a good female friend in your life. Try to find at least one female you can hang out with and get advice from.

Chapter 13 - Waitresses and bartenders work for tips

Have you ever noticed waitresses and female bartenders are often very friendly and nice to you? Do you feel flattered when they smile at you and give you lots of attention? Do you get all cocky and assume they think you're cute? Do you think they all want to fuck you? Don't be a dumbass. They work for tips. That is why they are being nice to you. They are trying to pay their rent and make their car payment every month. They have to convince men like you to leave them enough tips to cover all their expenses. The nicer they are to you, the more they get paid. Quite simply, "nice and flirty" equals "bigger tip".

That same waitress or bartender may also be thinking, "Maybe I can talk him into buying me a shot?" So, let me ask you, if you get the bartender drunk, is she going home with you because you got her drunk? Or is she going home with the guy that helped her clean up the bar after closing because she was too drunk to do it? My bet is the guy that helped her clean up.

So, quite bluntly, if you give waitresses and bartender's big tips and buy them drinks, someone else is going to benefit. It will not be you heading home with her at the end of the night. Don't waste your time and money buying drinks for cocktail waitresses and bartenders. There's no benefit in it for you. If it isn't going to help you get your dick wet, don't fucking do it! Now, as with most things in life, there are exceptions. There are times when you have a shot with one of these girls. Though rare, it does happen once in a blue moon or so. If you've done everything properly and managed to get yourself laid by the bartender just enjoy yourself. I'm certainly not going to hate on you.

If you really think she is into you, ask her for her phone number. Just don't be surprised if she tells you she has a boyfriend or is married. Take it as the "easy out" and move on. I was a frequent customer in a restaurant. I met a very cute waitress there. So every time I came to the restaurant, I asked for her section. She'd smile and flirt with me because she recognized me. She even called me by my first name. Finally, I asked her for her phone number, and she told me she had a boyfriend. Later, I realized she remembered me because I tend to tip her well. I highly doubt she had a boyfriend. Then again, that's okay with me. Yet another example of a time I recognized and took advantage of the easy out that was right in front of me. I've been to that restaurant several times since then. She has waited on me and it isn't awkward because I took that easy out. I still tip her well when I come in, and I will continue to because she's a damn good waitress. I won't however, ask for her number or try and find out if she's still with her "boyfriend".

Sometimes, though it is extremely rare, if you are a regular customer, a waitress may take the time to really get to know you. After some time goes by and she really starts to warm up to you, you might actually get a shot at taking her home. You'll only get one chance. Don't fuck it up. I went to the same bar frequently. I got to know many of the bartenders. One night after drinking heavily, I asked the bartender what she was doing when she got off work that night. She said, "Nothing, but I can't leave until after we finish cleaning up." I asked what time that was. She said 3:00 AM. So, I gave her my number and asked her to call me when she got off work. She called me at about 3:45 AM. Unfortunately, I fell asleep and slept through the call and the opportunity to have sex with her that night. The next time I went to the bar and saw her, I asked if she wanted to go out that night. She wasn't having it. She didn't want anything to do with me because she felt insulted that I hadn't answered the phone when she called me. Even though I apologized and explained to her I fell asleep when she called, she didn't care. I had my shot and missed it. Live and learn. Sometimes you only get one chance at a woman, so don't fuck it up.

Chapter 14 – A Whole New Opportunity Every 28 Days

If you screw up with a woman, remember that every 28 days yields a whole new opportunity. Don't get me wrong, if you fuck your girlfriend's mom and she catches you, don't even try to get back on her good side. You're a complete dumbass, and she's not going to want anything to do with you. But, if whatever you did to piss her off is a relatively minor infraction, you may be able to give it a few weeks' time and then reconcile. A woman's period resets the clock and her mindset. Let's put it this way. If you had to pee for three days non-stop, how thankful would you be after if finally stops? I'd be in a pretty good fucking mood!

Sometimes if you say the wrong thing at the wrong time and she doesn't want to talk to you, don't talk to her. Don't call her. Don't text or email her. Just stop dialing her digits, and leave her the hell alone for a while. A lot of the difference between doing well and not doing so well with women is simply all in your timing.

Wait two to three weeks and send her a simple, "Hello. Can we talk?" text message. If she responds in a positive way, and positive is NOT "Leave me the fuck alone!", then let her come to you. She may be thinking of you as well. But, sometimes you have to make the first move if you want to keep her in your life.

I'll share a personal example of how this played out in my own life a few years back. I was dating a woman and we were really into each other. We were having sex three to five times a week, and she was spending the night with me at least two times a week. She asked me after we'd both had a lot to drink one night, "Are you sleeping with anyone else?" Again, I had a lot to drink and wasn't thinking as clearly as I should have been. I said, "Well, no. But you know I was dating several women when we first started dating, right? But I'm not now." Yeah, that wasn't the right thing to say. She got really mad and didn't talk to me for about two weeks, maybe a little less than that. I sent her a text message stating, "I'd like to talk. I miss you." About an hour later, I got a message back stating, "I miss you too." That was all I needed to do and we started dating and having sex again just as we were before I'd fucked up and said something stupid.

Chapter 15 – When Women Move On

When a woman is thinking of dumping your ass, she has been looking for someone else long before she let you know it was over between the two of you. Women are like monkeys in this way. They always have another branch to grab on to before they let go of the current branch. Ever seen a monkey fall? If you have, it's probably because the branch they were clinging to broke. It is the same with women. Women won't let go of their man unless they have another dude lined up to take his place. She may not be actively seeing the guy, but she has definitely considered it.

If you are the guy asking a woman out and she says she has a boyfriend or a husband, it may or may not be true. Regardless, take the easy out. It may not be true but she may be trying to politely get rid of you. However, if it is true, be nice to her. She may be making a mental note to make you her boyfriend after she dumps the current one. She may also be testing you to see if you'd be a good fit for one of her friends. Or, she may not care about the current boyfriend or husband and you'll get your eyes fucked out later that night. Regardless, play it nice and cool. Just wait to see what happens.

If you are the guy with a woman who is looking to move on, I feel for you. You can't really stop that from happening. If she dumps you (especially if you lived together), ask her if she's seeing someone new. If she says she is seeing someone, walk away. She has already grabbed onto the new branch and is swinging on it.

If she says she is not seeing someone new, there are a few things to consider. She may be telling you the truth, for now. But, you can bet there is some other person she has shown an interest in. She is just waiting for that person to show an interest back in her. Then again, she may be lying to you and she really is seeing someone else. Who knows? But, you need to choose which option you want to go with.

You can choose to wait to see what the truth really is, and she may come back to you, or you can just fold your card game and walk away. Should you choose to wait, you should also know she will probably do the same thing to you again at some point in the future. I dated a woman and she dumped me. We made up a week later. The sex was great for a while, until she dumped me again. I chose to wait again, and she came back to me again. The sex was great again, until she dumped me a third time. Finally, I grew tired of this trend and moved on.

Chapter 16 – Separated and Newly Divorced Women

Women that are going through a divorce or have recently gone through a divorce are pretty predictable. They all have characteristics of one of a select few definable types and demeanors.

Women that are currently going through a divorce have two definable types. Type one is the scorned bitch, and type two is the fuck me woman. Of the two types, both are in confidence and self-esteem recovery mode. Neither type should be considered to be a long lasting relationship. Both are very temporary. Never enter into a relationship with a newly divorced or separated woman thinking you're going to be together forever and get engaged. It is not going to happen. Don't set yourself up for disappointment. Just enjoy the time with her for what it is, and leave it at that.

Why divorced and newly separated women are so easy differs from woman to woman. Some are looking for love, some for sex, some need a boost in their self-esteem, and some are just wired to be horny women.

I'm of the opinion that it doesn't matter why a woman has left her husband. I really don't care. She is now open for business in my book, and I'm not one to go looking for excuses to discourage a woman who wants to indulge in some sexual escapades.

Let's talk first about the type one woman. Type one women are scorned bitches. She may have been dumped and very possibly was cheated on. She is still hurting from the rejection. She appears to be cautious and reserved in her approach and demeanor. But, it usually isn't a reflection of how she is truly feeling inside. She won't date or have sex with you because, quite frankly, you're only around to help her regain her confidence.

Once she has that confidence back, you'll be history. A type one woman is just looking to kill time until she finds someone she really wants to date, or the guy that screwed her over comes back to her. She is probably still in love with him, but she really wants revenge because he's hurt her. You are nothing more than a tool for her to get revenge on this man and help boost her wounded self-esteem. However, if you're alright with being the tool, go for it. I find it to be a big waste of time though.

I've made this mistake before. I ended up spending my time and money on her and got nothing from her. As soon as a new guy came into her life, she dumped me. The funny thing about that is, when the new guy dumped her, she came running back to me. I was her doormat. If you run into a type one woman, just run away as fast and as far as you can go! It's not worth it no matter how hot she is.

Oh, and if you think you can use this woman to date her friends, it won't work either. Would you lend your doormat to a friend so that your friend's dog rubs his shit covered feet on it? I wouldn't. She won't either. You are her doormat. It is all about her, so the second you go for a friend of hers, she'll tell her friend a lot of bullshit about you, and then she'll dump your stupid ass.

If you really want to date a type one woman despite the fact it will probably be a disaster like a bad train wreck for you, I highly recommend you don't try to do anything with her on the first date. Don't get busy trying to get sexual with her right off the bat. Concentrate on the "no pressure" style to ensure a second date.

Start the second date by saying, "My only regret is I didn't have a chance to kiss you good night." If she responds with positive body language or agrees with you, you'll very likely get a kiss on the second date. Don't push for sex until a couple more dates later. She will let you know when she's ready for more. This method works well with type one women, but some still won't have sex with you until months later. But, if you are that into her, use your fucking hand and get used to it. Sometimes you're just so into a woman that you're willing to do what it takes.

Now, let's move on and take a look at the type two woman. Type two women have moved past the former relationship and are ready to move on. She is in search of the next branch to grab on to because she knows and has accepted that her relationship or marriage is over. She is moving on.

At this point, she's just waiting to find out how much money and assets will be awarded to her from the divorce. Type two women will have sex with you very quickly after you first meet them. She has needs and wants you to satisfy her, and so make sure you do. She'll insist on it.

Type two women are pretty aggressive sexually. I met one that had sex with me three times on the first date. She even brought over her favorite dildo so I would use it on her. She was more than willing to show me how she liked to use the dildo before she'd let me use it on her. If I counted correctly, she had seven orgasms that night. The sex was fantastic, but we didn't date for long.

We had a few nights of great sex and then the conversations started happening about a committed relationship. By the way, this was starting to happen after four dates. I knew I was the first guy she'd considered dating since her separation, plus I wasn't really all that into her. So I ended it. It's alright to get into a relationship with type two women. But, if you are the first guy she's dated since her separation, it won't last. Most therapists believe the first relationship after a separation will most likely fail. This is true for both men and women.

Type two women are reckless and heartless. You'll get laid and have good sex, but it won't last long. You also need to assume you are not the only man she is sleeping with. Don't fall in love with her, because she is probably cheating on you. I have a humorous example of this (Well, I think it's funny now.) I met a very cute blonde woman. I found out she was separated from her husband and out having fun and looking for men to date. My friend was talking to her friend, so it was very easy for me to get to know her.

After an interesting conversation, she and her friend decide to leave and go to the bar down the road. She asked if I could meet her there and dance with her for a few hours. I agreed. She left with her friend, and my friend and I stayed a few more minutes to finish our drinks, and then went to the other bar. I looked around for her. I found her in the corner with her tongue shoved down another man's throat. In short, if you meet a type two woman, take advantage of the situation because she wants you to, and you're certain to have some hot sex with her. But, move on quickly once you've had your fill, because she definitely will as soon as she finds another branch she's interested in swinging from if you get my drift.

Some women will talk about their ex-boyfriend or ex-husband constantly. I think that is pretty self-explanatory. If she talks about him, she's still thinking about him. It could mean she hates the guy, but does it really matter? He's still on her mind. I dated a woman that kept bringing up her ex. I slept with her and once we were done having sex, the first thing she stated was, "My ex used to touch me like that when we had sex." My response to her was, "You know what, I really don't fucking care." That was the last time I saw her, and that was just fine by me. It's rude and annoying as hell to sit and talk about your ex all of the time. I was glad to move on and not have to listen to her drone on and on about this dude constantly.

Sometimes it can be challenging to recognize what type of woman she is. You'll have to watch out for the standard signs we covered in the earlier chapters. Watch her body language. If she sits in a closed position, she is a bit uptight and probably a type one. If she sits close to you and isn't afraid to touch you, she is most likely a type two.

The exception to the rule is women that are just starting to date after amicably ending a relationship. She is not a type one nor a type two. She will show interest but move very slowly. Just show an interest in her and she'll respond.

Chapter 17 – Touching and Kissing

You should know this by now, unless you have never touched a woman. Women like to be touched. I know, shocking right! When you touch her, don't rub or touch the same spot more than three to four times consecutively. She is not a fucking board, and you aren't trying to sand her down. Touch her and move to the next spot.

The time of the year matters as well. If it is the winter, touch her and take a mental note of her temperature. If it feels warm to you, then you feel cold to her. She won't want to be colder in the winter than she already is. Move to a spot that is cold to you so it feels warm to her. If you can't find a spot, go run your hands under hot water before you touch her again or she'll kick your ass out of the bed. If it is the summer, do just the opposite.

If you find an area that is warm to your touch, it will feel cool and refreshing to her. The key word here is warm. If you find an area that is hot to your touch, move on. If it's hot to you, your touch is ice cold to her. That'll get the wrong reaction from the one you are going for. I'll make this really simple for you. If she jumps, screams, punches you, or runs away, you won't get laid. So, if you see any of those reactions, you didn't do it right.

Touching and kissing can sometimes be the same because you can use your tongue instead of your hands and fingers. However, it is a different way to touch that is always the same temperature and not rough and dry like hands can get at times. The first thing you need to do is find where she is ticklish. It varies from woman to woman, but I usually find a good spot around the ears and neck. If you kiss her ears, don't breathe heavily into them. It makes you sound like a cow, and that isn't really a turn on for her. I've found many interesting spots. Some women like to have the back of their neck kissed all the way into the hairline. Others like the spot right under the arm by the armpit but not in the armpit. There are many. Back of the knees, toes, ankle, inner thigh, nipples, lower back right above the ass, etc.

The point is, you have to figure it out. She won't tell you where all her sensitive spots are. Well, she may, but it's always fun to find them on your own anyway. In reality, she may not even be aware of the sensitive spot until you find it. All you have to do is listen to her and watch her. You'll know right away by her pleasant reaction if you hit one of the right spots. Watch her body language. If she moves or moans, that is good. If she does nothing, move to another spot. However, if she does nothing and you've pretty much kissed or licked every inch of her, get your clothes on and run away! She will be terrible in bed.

Don't keep kissing the same spot. This is the same rule as touching. Remember, you aren't kissing yourself in the mirror. You have a woman next to you to explore. Go explore! The only rule I follow is, if it smells bad, don't kiss it. It won't taste good, and then you'll be turned off.

Don't give her wet sloppy kisses on her body. How would you like it if she drooled in your belly button? Keep it moist, but not gross and wet.

Watch out for the game players. If she plays the game, "Find my tickle spots, but I won't tell you where they are or when you've found them", imagine your life with her. Think about that. How about, "I'm mad at you but I won't tell you why." Or, "I think you're a jerk, but I'm not telling you why." I have had women play that game. It gets old really quickly. The game is "reward and punishment." Let's put it this way. Any way you play that game, she is rewarded because she gets to punish you. When I was with a woman that played that game, I was always wondering, "What the hell did I do to deserve that?" I never figured it out. It ended, and I am absolutely thrilled it did.

When you start out, start with softly touching her body with your lips. It should be so soft that it tickles your lips. Keep in mind, that you are always being judged by a woman when you're getting to know her. She is going to judge you on how you'd be for a lover when you're kissing her. Many women enjoy foreplay more than sex.

I was dating a cute blonde that loved to be touched and kissed everywhere. One night I got especially playful and she had ten orgasms before we had sex and two more during sex. She was rare because she could actually have an orgasm from sucking on her nipples. Though, I'd do one better by sucking on her nipples and playing with her clit at the same time.

Many women also consider kissing as sex. To them, full blown sex is your reward for good foreplay. I once dated a woman who let me touch and kiss her body but she wouldn't have sex with me. I bluntly asked if she was ready to have sex with me. She stunned me when she said, "What do you mean? We are having sex!" I dated another woman that made her decision of whether she was going to sleep with a man by how he kissed. She slept with me so, I passed the test. She was very into foreplay. She expected a lot of kissing and foreplay and in return, she would give me sex. However, after sex, she required her reward of after play. Some women like after play. Some women absolutely love after play. This woman loved it. After play is really nothing more than touching and kissing after sex. She liked to have me touch her and caress her body until she fell asleep. Touching her like this made her feel like she had a complete sexual experience.

Chapter 18 – So... You've Been Dumped

This is one of those chapters that I could write a book on all by itself. Getting dumped is horrible. It makes you feel hopeless and worthless. However, take comfort in the fact that it happens to everyone. Anyone that decides to take the chance of getting to know another takes the risk of rejection, and it fucking hurts when it happens. However, you may not realize this at the moment, but you really have a great opportunity here. The sleeper has awakened!

The first rule you never ever, ever want to break, (which I have broken and regret all to hell) is do not ever date a woman that is like your ex-girlfriend or ex-wife. Here's my story. I had a wife that thought the money I made was hers to spend. She was very high maintenance. I met a lovely woman after the divorce that had a huge chest and pretty jet black hair. She was also high maintenance but claimed to be low maintenance. I got really into her. She was exactly what I thought I needed. Until she dumped me because she had never been married and I never wanted to get married again. The reality is, I started to fall for a woman that had the same tendencies my ex-wife had. Don't be a dumbass. Don't make that mistake. It fucking sucks. If you find yourself dating someone like the woman you were married to or dated in the past, get the fuck out! Do it now! Don't think about it, just do it. You are working in your comfort zone and you shouldn't be. I understand though. You understand that type of person and can ask them out easily. You know that type of woman and you can easily understand them. I get that. However, don't be a fucking dumbass. You should stretch and meet other women that have different tendencies you might like more. For example, I've met women that are very vocal about what they like in bed. I love that. She told me how she likes to cum, and I like to make that happen. Call me a team player! But, that turns me on. My high maintenance ex-wife was a bit of a prude. She wouldn't help me at all. Fuck that! I like sex. I love it when a woman has an orgasm or several. I'm not psychic. I can't read minds. Help me out here!

The second rule involves sabotaging the newly failed relationship. We've all done this at some point. But, if you just got dumped, you may want to say mean things or do malicious things to piss her off. Truthfully, this is really not helpful to anyone, especially you. Let's put it this way. When you got dumped, you probably had some inclination it was going to happen. We all have that weird vibe something isn't right.

Let me give you an example. I was dating a woman that told me she didn't like the fact that I had been married before. She herself had never been married. She spent the night with me several times after that, but was obviously bothered by something.

I'm going to divert for a second from the story and tell you something I've learned about children. If a child continually asks the same question over and over again, they didn't like the answer you gave them the other times they asked. You have to figure out what answer the child is really looking for and answer it in the way the child understands. A woman is a child in some ways.

The woman I was dating brought up a concern about my previous marriage and I didn't answer it in a way she liked. Women are different from children because they won't continually ask until they get the answer they want to here. You have one shot. If you say the wrong thing, her body language will tell you. If she is a vocal woman, her voice will tell you and the whole fucking room. Regardless, I knew I was going to get dumped at some point because I saw her behavior change. So, when it happened, she asked if we could continue to be friends. I told her no. I was very mean to her. I was an asshole. I knew what I was doing. I really knew that dating her was not going to work so I had to make sure she wouldn't come back to me. So, I was an asshole to her. Don't be an asshole. Just move on. It looks better for you. Plus, if you go graciously, you may be able to score on one of her friends that may be into you that you didn't know about before. If her friend knows you got dumped and were not an asshole about it, that works in your favor. Women tend to like guys that aren't assholes. Take the easy out and move on.

I'm going to state the obvious here, but because you just got dumped, the last thing you should be looking for is another relationship. I've met women that do that. It's some fucked up weird way of getting back what they lost. Be a man. Get over being dumped by having random sex with women and hold on finding a new relationship. A relationship is the last thing you need. If you decide to find a new relationship, you'll probably find a woman that has the same tendencies as your ex and end up getting dumped again. Instead, go out and stretch. I suppose I should explain what I mean by "stretching".

I call this "stretching" because it forces you to be more social and intimate with other women. It's a good exercise to do because it gets your mind off your ex and you get laid too! Purposely try to meet women that are different ages and personalties that your ex was. When I was 35, I slept with a 49 year old woman. She became a very good friend to me. She loved sex and was more than willing to have it with me. Her and I are still friends today and occasionally have sex. We're both fine with that. My ex's were all close to my age. I stretched and enjoyed a woman older and way more sexually experienced than I was.

As another example, my ex was not into exercising, though she was thin. I met a woman that was heavily into Yoga. Until I met her, I didn't really know what Yoga was. After dating her, I really like Yoga women. I've found that they are very flexible! This has become one of my regular dating questions when I meet new women. If she says she is into yoga, she is already starting to interest me.

If your, soon to be, ex-wife dumped you, I can relate. I was the dumpee in my marriage. I have advice for you on that too. If you aren't divorced yet, but ready to meet new women, lie! I normally don't advise lying. Wait, yes I do! Lie your ass off. Tell them you are divorced or you'll never even get to first base.

However, make sure you act like you are really divorced. Women can somehow sense the rejection of you getting dumped. You need to put on a good show. To do that, don't ever talk about your ex. Did you miss the part about it being about her? If so, you need to pay better attention.

There's only one acceptable time to talk about your ex, in therapy where no other women can here you complain. If the conversation comes up, she may ask why the two of you broke up. Just tell her, "We grew apart and went our own ways. We don't even talk anymore." That tells her you end relationships peacefully and on a good note. If she pushes harder on the topic, and she will, you need to divert it back to her. It can be tough, but get the conversation back to her. Again, the less she knows about you, the better. Nothing personal, but all men are dumbasses. Just shut your fucking mouth and let her talk.

Chapter 19 – Asking Her Out

When you here the phrase "Timing is everything", believe it. It holds true with women too. If you ask a woman out and your timing is off, she'll say no. If your timing is REALLY bad, she'll probably tell you to fuck off! Wait for the right time. It takes a little practice to figure out when the right time is. Generally, it is best to ask her face to face. That way, you can pick up on her body language.

If she's smiling when you come near her, ask her out. Remember, she is attempting to pick up on your body language as well. She is going to attempt to read your face to see if you are asking her out because you like her or just because you want to fuck her. Smile like you just saw a long lost best friend. Even if you are just asking her out to have sex with her, smile and be very positive.

If she isn't smiling, don't ask her out. I've asked women out when they aren't smiling just to see what the reaction is. I've heard, "Who the fuck do you think you are?" and "Does it LOOK like I want to go out with you?" I find it funny so I often do that for fun! It becomes even more amusing when I respond, "That's OK. I was asking only because I felt bad for you." I don't suggest doing that, by the way. It is always best to take the easy out and just say, "No problem. Thank you anyway." You never know, she may feel badly about how she reacted and come apologize to you. I have had that happen as well. I approached a woman and she somewhat smiled. So, I asked her out. She replied, "Get the fuck away from me!" So I apologized about interrupting her and walked away. About an hour later, she walked up to me and apologized. She still wasn't interested in me but she introduced me to three of her friends. One of which was interested in me much to my delight.

If you think you can ask a woman out over a note, email, or text message, ask yourself, "Am I still ten years old?" Women can't get an emotional read from you if you ask them out in written form. She will want to size up your intentions. I have asked women out in text messages, and they've said yes. However, when (and if) we went out, she sized me up right away and automatically assumed I asked her out in a text message only to get laid. Who knows, at the time you texted her and asked her out, she might have only wanted sex from you. Now that time has passed, her intentions have probably changed. The odds are strongly against you getting your dick wet, but as always, there is a small chance.

You can ask a woman out over the phone. However, you should have met in person at least once before making that phone call. If you haven't met, it is the same as texting her out. How can she determine your intentions by listening to your voice? If you've met her, she's heard your voice and had a discussion with you. She can then somewhat determine your intentions over the phone. She will probably go out with you but you'll be sized up for at least the first half of the date.

Women are brought up to think the worst of you for asking them out. Even in today's sexual standards, I don't know too many parents that teach their daughters to sleep with every man that asks her out. Instead, most parents attempt to teach their children to be safe and wary of the opposite sex. That holds true for boys and girls now. However, now that she is an adult and has experience with men, she is probably even more wary of men then she was as a teenager.

Chapter 20 – Dress Code for Dating

Guys let's face it, if you dress like a dumbass, you won't get far. What you're wearing speaks volumes to women. Even from a distance, she'll look at you and start making a decision whether she is even going to talk to you. If your gear is sharp, she'll start to ask herself if you are someone she'd want to be seen with by her peers. If she answers her own question with a "no", you may still get laid for the night, but that's about it.

For example, never wear all black. You'll look like a butler or a waiter. Hell, someone may even stop you and ask you to get them a drink! Never wear a short sleeved shirt with a buttoned front on it. Only computer geeks wear those. (No offense to the techie's reading this, of course!) Don't wear your work clothes unless they are top of the line clothing. If you're a painter, don't wear your clothes you just wore to work and got all messy. If you're a CEO for a corporation, you're probably wearing a suit and tie most of the time to work. That would be fine to wear. Most men only buy clothes for work. If you aren't a CEO, kick your dating gear up a notch.

Here are some ideas for you. You'll need a couple different items because you can't wear the same outfit every time you go out. If a woman sees you two nights in a row wearing the same outfit, she may be interested the first night but certainly won't be on the second night. She'll probably think you're too poor to buy yourself decent cloths and avoid you like the plague.

Buy yourself a pair of good fitting jeans and boots to wear with a dress shirt. Wear this outfit to a bar that everyone else is dressed business casual. This will help you stand out from the rest and still look sharp. It's okay to stand out from the rest a little bit, just don't go overboard.

Buy a business class suit and wear this on the nights you're going to a high end restaurant. You can wear the suit to the bars that everyone else is dressed business casual as well. Just remember to take the suit coat off when you sit down. This makes you look more approachable.

Buy a couple of high end excellent quality dress shirts, pants, and shoes. The shirts are worth the extra money as they'll last longer and tend to be more comfortable. Wear this outfit to a bar where everyone else is wearing jeans and boots. Again, this will make you stand out a bit in a good way.

Be more noticeable than the other guys but not weird. You are presenting yourself to the world to be noticed and admired, not to annoy or anger. Feel good about what you're wearing and be confident.

If you're not sure about what to wear or how to pick out your new dating gear, make friends with a woman. It is preferable that it be a co-worker or someone you can't have sex with for various reasons. She should be someone you wouldn't mind going out with but she's happily married or already dating someone. Once you have your woman friend, ask her to go shopping with you. Most women love to shop, and you'll probably have a lot of fun as she dresses you up in all sorts of new gear. As an added perk, she may really like how you look in your new clothes and hook you up with one of her friends. One key point to mention is, when you're out with your woman friend, act like a friend. Do not make any advances on her, or you'll fuck this all up. Treat her like your best friend and she'll help you out.

I had a great female friend that I asked to help me pick out new clothing. She did and to my surprise, shortly after buying and wearing my new clothes, I met a woman that had similar looks and tastes. I like to take my friend out to lunch and let her pick the place. She'd always take me to places where there were lots of other women of her looks and style.

Chapter 21 – It's All About Them

If you're in a conversation with a beautiful woman, you should tell her everything about you, right? Wrong! So very wrong! Steer the conversation to be about them. If, at the end of the night, she doesn't know much about you then you did it right. She really doesn't care to know about you. She wants to be understood by you. If you don't understand her, make sure you give her the impression that you do.

The older women get, the more they want to share their issues with you and know you're alright with the issues. In this case, steer the conversation to having her tell you positive things she currently enjoys in her life. Younger women just want to have fun so steer the conversation to the fun things she's done or wants to do.

If you start talking about yourself, you'll lose her interest. Men build their self-esteem up by who will take the time to listen to them. Women build their self-esteem by having others show and interest in what they think. Let's face it. Women will rate you on a scale of one to ten.

A one sucks while a ten rocks out loud. You will be rated higher if you show interest in her and shut up about yourself.

Sometimes, the conversation turns negative. Don't contribute to the conversation if she is complaining about her friends or family. It's alright for her to trash them, but not you. If you do, she'll almost immediately stick up for them, and you'll become the bad guy. Use words like "wow", "really", "Ok," "Hmm", and the phrase, "How did that make you feel?" Then, try to change the topic to something light and fun. Do your best to have her talking in a positive manner.

Women are all about feelings. If she is angry at someone and telling you about it, she will remember you in the future by the mood she was in and feelings she was having. Don't associate yourself with a trash can! If she is negative and talking to you negatively, steer the conversation to a positive tone. Try to get her laughing. You want her remembering the positive conversation, not the negative.

If she starts to cry and talk about her past, move on. You just crossed the line to being someone she just wants to talk to. I had someone yell at me as if she was talking to her old boyfriend once! I couldn't get away fast enough! Some women are just looking for a shoulder to cry on or someone to fill the male role so they can pretend you're their boyfriend or dad.

Here is an example of one of the wrong conversations I had.

HER: "I've been divorced twice, and I'll never marry again."
ME: "I've been divorced once."
She walked away. The reason why is because the conversation changed to me.

Here is an example of a good conversation I've had.

ME: "What do you do for a living?"
HER: "I'm a hair stylist."
ME: "I like your hair."
HER: "Thank you!"
ME: "I'm protesting bad haircuts!"
HER: She laughed and said, "Ohh, that's sad!"
ME: "Yeah. No, not really. I'm a rebel! What do you like best about your job?"
HER: She laughed again and said, "I like meeting new people."
ME: "Well, I'm glad I met you. You're good at it!"
HER: She laughed again and said, "Me too." Then she smiled.

This conversation shows how I steered the conversation to her I learned what she did for a living and what she liked best about it. I made her laugh and kept it very positive. It all started because I know hair stylists have a passion for fashionable haircuts and styles. As a result, I focused on that, and we had a good conversation and had sex that night.

Long story short, you need to find out things about her and talk about them but leave things about you out of the conversation. Ask questions. She may ask you questions. Answer them simply and get her talking about herself again as quickly as possible.

Chapter 22 – Dating Requirement Questions

As time goes on, you'll start dating more and more. I started dating five women at the same time. I could only maintain that for a couple weeks and fucked up one night and called one woman a different name. Yeah, I got dumped right after that! However, you'll start to meet women with traits and qualities you really like and others you dislike. I ask several questions and if they answer incorrectly, they make it to my "sex only" list.

Here are my questions:

Do you like sushi?

If yes, she gets a point.

If no, she loses a point.

Have you ever tried Yoga? If so, do you like it?

If yes, she gets a point.

If no, she loses a point.

Who paid for your car? (You need to know if her ex or her daddy paid for the car. Trust me on this one.)

If she paid for car, she gets a point. It means she takes care of herself.

If her ex or her father paid for car, she loses a point. She wants a sugar daddy.

How do you get along with your dad?

If she gets along with him, she gets a point.

If she doesn't, she loses a point. If she has problems with her dad, she could be looking for someone to fill in for him until she gets the issue resolved. One of my friends advised me, "It will only work until one of you get healthy."

What is your mom like? Let's face it. Women tend to follow in their mom's footsteps. There is an extremely good chance you'll be seeing the same behaviors her mom has. My ex-wife showed rebellion to her mom when we were dating and ended up exactly like her mom in the end.

Many women will get along great with you until they become a mom. At that point, everything changes for them and they end up becoming their mom. Well, that is what they say growing up. "You become your mom." I live by another phrase as well, "Look at the mother because that is really who you will be dating in the future." This is sooo true! On a related side note, if a woman asks something and somewhere in the sentence uses the word "so" then she is hiding a question you are answering for them but they are not asking. For example, let's say you were to ask her, "Are you going to be a bitch someday?" She may answer, "My mom's a bitch. So, I don't know how dad put up with her." Translation, she will most likely go down the same path as her mother.

One other thing I make sure to take notice of while I'm out somewhere eating with her. I don't ask this question, this is more obvious than anything else. How does she eat her food? If I haven't already slept with her, this tells me how she'll be in bed. If she is picky with her food, she'll be picky on what she'll let you do to her body.

I dated a woman that was beautiful but very picky with her food. It had to be expensive and top of the line. One night we went out and I was in her driveway. I couldn't stay the night because of work commitments so I started fingering her. She kissed me and said, "Goodnight." I said, "Shut up and cum for me."

She got very angry, stepped out of the car, and walked away. The next day, she dumped me because I was coarse and blunt. It didn't fit with her expensive and "refined" style.

Continuing on with the topic of eating with a woman... If the woman eats slowly and enjoys the food, she'll greatly enjoy foreplay. If she eats fast and gorges herself, she'll just fuck you over and over and cum repetitively. If she always wants what others are having, run. Run fast! She'll always be looking for your replacement. On a side note unrelated to eating but similar in a way, if she turns the radio station a lot and can't keep to a single song or a cd, she is always going to be looking for a better deal. You are on the way out.

Chapter 23 – Questions You WILL be Asked You SHOULD Know How to Answer

As in the last chapter about your prerequisite dating questions, women will have some for you. It is important to know the correct way to answer these because if you answer wrong, your ass is dumped. What's worse, you won't get laid tonight! Some of the questions are easy to answer, others are not. For example, if a woman asks you, "How old do you think I am?" Yeah, you should lie! I met this woman that appeared to be 25ish and I was 35ish. She asked me that question and I thought it would be funny to go up in age rather than down. I answered, "40 maybe 50." She gave me a really shitty look, turned, and walked away quickly. Remember my friend Joe? He was with me that night. He looked at me and said, "Dude! Never ever talk about age, and if you do, guess low!" He finished by calling me a "dumb fuck." He was right. That was a dumb ass thing to do. I was trying to be funny. It didn't work.

Here is another question that will pop up as well. "Have you ever cheated on someone you were dating?" Let's face it. She's asking because she wants to know if you're going to cheat on her. She has probably been cheated on in the past and is still feeling pissed off about it.

If you are a cheater, whether you got busted for it or not, lie. If you answer this question honestly, you're punted. The other much less likely occurrence is, she'll fuck you hard for the night but won't call you the next day. You'll be viewed as a "short term" guy. If you aren't a cheater, answer honestly. If a woman cheated on you, tell her that is why you don't cheat and why you think it is wrong, even if you don't really think that way.

If she asks, "Why are you not dating someone right now?" This girl has self-esteem issues. She is asking to attempt to determine your flaws. Basically, she is looking for a reason not to date you any longer. She is interested in you, but wants to know why the others you dated are no longer interested in you. If you are dating someone at this moment, she obviously doesn't know. Don't be a dumbass and say, "Oh, I am. What? You thought you were the only one?" Lie. Tell her you are not dating anyone and the reason is only because you are very selective about whom you get close to. If you really aren't dating anyone and haven't for a while, don't appear desperate. Say something cute like, "I'm not dating anyone because I hadn't met you until now!"

Here is one of my favorites. "What do you like to do for fun?" She's curious to know if you have a hobby that will take up a lot of your time and make it so you'll spend less time with her. For example, some women really hate football season. If you're a huge football fan, it may bother her because she knows you'll be at games or in front of the television all the time during the season. So, it really isn't a good idea to tell her you have season tickets to your favorite team. At least, not unless you plan on taking her with you to the games.

Answer this question with something you like doing, but doesn't take an abundance of your time. For example, I like to brew my own beer and make my own wine. I usually will tell her I do both because she probably doesn't realize how long it can take to brew a batch of beer and I usually leave that information out. I also tell her I like to ride my bike and go for walks. This tells her I like to be outside and it's something she could do with me.

The next question will be asked if she is half way interested in you. "What do you do for a living?" It sounds like a simple question to answer. It isn't. This is a loaded question. She is fishing for a few things with this one. She wants to know how much money you make without asking you straight up. She wants to know if you have the potential of being a good provider to her. She also wants to know if you're a responsible person or a partier.

If you have a good job you are proud of, tell her the truth but be very vague. Remember, she is not really interested in hearing you talk. Try to shift the conversation back to her as quickly as possible. If you have a shitty job, lie and tell her you're a lawyer. There are so many of them now that it'll be believable. By all means, don't tell her about your shitty job. If you start down the negative conversation path, you won't get out and you're not going to get laid.

Some women just get right to the point. She may ask, "Are you just looking to get laid?" Or, it could be some variation of this question. I've been asked this using many words like "hook up", "fuck", and "use me for sex". There are many ways this question will be asked which also makes it a tough question to answer. Yeah, the answer is, we're guys. We always want to have sex! Since she is asking this question, she may already know the answer and just want you to admit it. In this case, say something like, "Yes, but only because you think I'm sexy!" Make a joke out of it. Other times, this is a legitimate question she is concerned about. This is a good thing. She is interested in the sex being a repeat occurrence.

I have had a surprising number of women ask me the next question. "Why did you ask me to dance?" In this case, she really wants to know what you want from her. She is asking herself if you're looking for a one night stand or looking for something longer term. She is curious about you. Women always have a plan and she's trying to figure out what your plan is. Answer her question like this, "The way you move to the music compelled me to come over and dance with you." By all means, if you're buddies literally pushed you over there to talk with her because you are chicken, don't tell her that!

Chapter 24 – Faux Pas

As there are questions you need to ask her and questions she may ask you, there are questions you should NEVER EVER ask. You may have asked one or more of these questions already. If you did, you should know better than to ask them again. Let's start with the biggest one first.

Never ask a woman, "Do you love me?" Are you kidding man? Seriously? Unless you plan on telling her you love her, don't ask her this question! I was drinking heavily with a woman I was dating. We were lying in bed naked and I playfully asked her if she loved me. She replied, "I really care for you." And, to be honest, I was fine with that. I was half drunk after all. I replied, "Good." She didn't seem bothered at the time. Two days later, she dumped me. In truth, she may have dumped me for more than just this, but it definitely had a hand in it.

One of the dumbest questions to ask a woman is, "Do you want to fuck?" Well, now she knows you only want sex. Great job genius! Women don't want to put a gross name to sex.

Many women don't like the word "Fuck". I have found women that use that word are coarse and blunt. If they use it in everyday conversations, run away! Don't be her next baby daddy! If they use it between you and her only, she's kinky and has accepted having sex with you is a good fun thing to do. Avoid this question and just go do her. On a humorous note, a friend of mine and I had a bet to see if one of us could take a woman home after starting the conversation with this question. Neither of us got laid that night and I had a bruise on my face from getting slapped so many times! It was a crazy night though.

The biggest question of all to avoid is, "Do you want to get married?" What? Are you nuts? If you ask a woman that question, you better be wanting that yourself! She will never let it drop if you ask her this question. It'll come up over and over until you go totally ape shit crazy. What worse is she'll think you want to get married. Within a month of asking her, she'll expect a ring. I have dated women that asked me this and my reply is, "I've done that once and have no desire to do it again!" It sounds harsh but it stops the question from being asked again.

I strongly suggest to not ask, "Are you on your period?" She probably is on it and embarrassed about it. Women don't enjoy that time of the month and certainly don't broadcast when they are. If she is being bitchy, just assume she is on her period or that she is mad at you about something. Keep your mouth shut! I have asked that question myself. She was on her period. That was a given. I asked anyway because she was being an absolutely self-righteous bitch! Her response was, "You assume I'm on my period just because I'm having a bad day? Don't you have bad days? Who do you think you are making assumptions about me when you have no clue how my day was?" Yeah, I slept on the couch that night.

Chapter 25 - So You're Married and NOT Getting Any Sex

You've been married for a while now and, in the beginning, you got a shit ton of sex. Now, you are getting older and not getting sex at all or very little, with the exception of some excessive masturbating. If self-pleasure isn't cutting it for you, you need to take a serious look at yourself. Even though you are married and in a presumably committed relationship, you need to bait the hook for the fish you're trying to catch. In other words, get in shape and get your dating skills ready for a workout. Make yourself presentable and, by all means, don't stink. When you dress like shit and smell worse, your wife isn't going to want to touch you! If you're drinking too much alcohol, drink less. If you're smoking too much, smoke less. If you're a fat slob, eat less. Once you get yourself back into the grove you were in when you were dating or newlyweds, she'll pick up on that and your bed will start to see some action again.

If none of that works for you, she may have something physically wrong with her that is lowering her libido. She should see a doctor if this is the problem. However, do not ask her if something is wrong with her sex drive or you'll have one really pissed off wife. She needs to realize it herself so she can accurately talk with a doctor about the problem.

The easiest way I'd suggest to go about helping her realize the issue is by making a move on her every night until she hears herself tell you, "I'm not in the mood." If she says that enough, she'll eventually bring it up to you. In the short term, get yourself some porn and whack it. It'll take a while for her to come to the realization that she may have something wrong with her.

The other possibility is that she is sleeping with another guy. This is usually pretty apparent, as she'll be gone a lot and on the phone a lot where you can't overhear. If she is really into the other guy, your time is short with her anyway so you'll be getting a divorce soon enough. So, as I stated before, bait the hook for fish you are trying to catch. Get back into shape and maybe you'll hit the dating scene all ready to start getting your dick wet again. And, who knows, once you're back in shape, she may dump the other guy and start over with you. Be careful with this though. If she is really just

trying to plan a birthday party for you, you don't
want to look like an ass.

Chapter 26 – Conclusion

We have covered a lot in this book. You should, by now, understand that women are very sexual. They want sex too and they like it. Yes, you have some that never have an orgasm, but even they like the action as well. Every woman is different and wants different things. After reading this book, you have the raw truth you need to understand better what to expect in the dating world. Don't get me wrong, you need a lot of practice. Even the seasoned super studs that sleep with a different woman every night mess up. My buddy has sex with a different woman almost every night. I laughed my ass off the other day because he made move on a woman and she literally punched him in the jaw! Yeah, he screwed up.

I hope you take away a lot from this book whether you are a man or a woman. Women, remember to look me up and have loud screaming sex with me! Otherwise, I hope this book lets you understand how a man sees the dating scene. We are just trying to figure out what you want from us so we can see you naked! Just remember, if you're into the guy, help him through it. If you aren't, punt him quickly and get it over with. Men, remember to think with your head, not your dick. That isn't always easy, but possible. If you find a woman that's into you, hopefully she helps you out and doesn't make it too difficult for you to get her cookie.

Richard Master

I am glad you enjoyed, *Sex Up Your Life* and I hope you are getting laid a lot more now. I am Richard Master. I am just a regular guy. I'm not a supermodel. But, I've spent my adult life trying to figure out and understand women. I have learned and continue to learn over time. Women want to be appreciated. Sometimes, appreciation equates to bondage and whips. Other times is equates to shutting your mouth and listening. I have friends that have helped me along the way and now I'm passing the knowledge on to you. I want you to succeed. I want you to get your dick wet way more often than you do now. My life experience and the shared experiences of my friends can help you gain an edge on the other guys you're competing against. After all, you both want to score. The real question is, "Who will she let into her pants?"

My knowledge has been from ***thousands*** of attempts to meet and have sex with women. The majority of my attempts have failed for various reasons, but when I stick to what I've said in this book, I succeed a lot more often! Getting rejected when talking to a woman is not necessarily a bad thing. Embrace it. I've learned to like it as it gets me fueled up to try again and again.

A SPECIAL THANK YOU TO YOU!

On behalf of everyone at Freedom Of Speech Publishing, thank you for choosing Sex Up Your Life for your reading enjoyment.

As an added bonus and special thank you, for purchasing Sex Up Your Life, you can enjoy discounts and special promotions on other Freedom of Speech Publishing products. Visit www.freedomeofspeech.com/vip to learn more.

We are committed to providing you with the highest level of customer satisfaction possible. If for any reason you have questions or comments, we are delighted to hear from you. Email us at cs@freedomofspeechpublishing.com or visit our website at: http://freedomofspeechpublishing.com/contact-us-2/.

If you enjoyed Sex Up Your Life, visit www.freedomofspeechpublishing.com for a list of similar books or upcoming books.

Again, thank you for your patronage. We look forward to providing you more entertainment in the future.

Sex Up Your Life
By Richard Master

For more books like this one, visit Richard Master's website at:

http://richardmaster.com/

Printed in the United States of America
The publisher offers discounts on this book when ordered in bulk quantities. For more information, contact Sales Department, Phone 815-290-9605, Email:
sales@FreedomOfSpeechPublishing.com

Freedom of Speech Publishing, Leawood KS, 66224
www.FreedomOfSpeechPublishing.com
ISBN: 193863408X
ISBN-13: 978-1-938634-08-6